The Light That Is Given

The Light That Is Given

Prophetic Quaker Faith

PATRICIA DALLMANN

RESOURCE *Publications* • Eugene, Oregon

THE LIGHT THAT IS GIVEN
Prophetic Quaker Faith

Copyright © 2024 Patricia Dallmann. All rights reserved. Except for brief quotations in critical publications or reviews, no part of this book may be reproduced in any manner without prior written permission from the publisher. Write: Permissions, Wipf and Stock Publishers, 199 W. 8th Ave., Suite 3, Eugene, OR 97401.

Resource Publications
An Imprint of Wipf and Stock Publishers
199 W. 8th Ave., Suite 3
Eugene, OR 97401

www.wipfandstock.com

PAPERBACK ISBN: 979-8-3852-1993-3
HARDCOVER ISBN: 979-8-3852-1994-0
EBOOK ISBN: 979-8-3852-1995-7

All rights reserved. No part of this book may be reproduced or transmitted in any form or by any means, electronic, mechanical, including photocopying, recording, or by any information storage and retrieval system, without permission in writing from the publisher.

Scripture is quoted from the King James Version of the Bible, copyright 1990 by Thomas Nelson Publishers.

Scripture is quoted from the New English Bible, copyright 1971 by Cambridge University Press and Oxford University Press.

Scripture is quoted from the New Testament translated by Richmond Lattimore, copyright 1996 by Alice B. Lattimore.

Is not the way of life, the way of holiness, the way of truth, the way of peace, one and the same in all ages and generations? Was there ever, or shall there ever be another than that which was from the beginning?
—Isaac Penington

Contents

Introduction | ix
A Colony of Heaven | 1
Questionnaire | 3
Each Gives Out of His Store | 9
Partaking of the Sufferings | 10
The Ubiquitous War of the Lamb | 18
Doing Our Part | 23
The Only Antidote | 27
Dynamics of Evil | 35
The Rose That Bare Gesù | 39
The Mediate Role of Virtue | 40
In Him We Live, Move, and Have Our Being | 43
On Presumption and Belief in John 11 | 51
On Redemption in John 11 | 58
Some Observations on John's Second Epistle | 63
Some Observations on Revelation 10:5–7 | 67
Increase our Faith: Some Observations on Luke 17:1–10 | 70
His Seed Remaineth | 75
The Solitary Ascent | 78
Powers of the Soul | 83
Enduring unto the End | 86
Opening Scriptures: Parable of the Wheat and Tares | 89
Shooting the Moon: An Essay on Reflection and Substance | 94
As I Have Loved You | 97
Hear Ye Him: Some Observations on Matthew 17 | 100
The Inward Eclipse | 103
Called To Christ | 105

Contents

Moses and the Burning Bush | 107
The New Way | 109
Sifting the Heart: Some Observations on the Second Chapter of Matthew | 111
Righteousness Fulfilled: Some Observations on the Third Chapter of Matthew | 115
The Mind of Christ | 118
Introduction to Lewis Benson Lectures | 123
    Introduction to "The Power of the Gospel" | 123
    Introduction to "The Gospel and Self-Knowledge" | 124
    Introduction to "The Place of George Fox in Christian History" | 127
    Introduction to "The Everlasting Gospel Preached by George Fox" | 129
    Introduction to "The Relation of Fox's Message to the Bible" | 130
    Introduction to "The New Worship" | 130
    Introduction to "The New Ministry" | 132
    Introduction to "Restoring the Church of the Cross" | 133
    Introduction to "The Christian Universalism of George Fox" | 135
Dialogue on Quaker Understanding of Free Will | 138
Dialogue on Old Testament Stories | 145
Dialogue on Importance of Covenants | 148
A Conversation on Faith | 153
Review of *Traditional Quaker Christianity* | 159

Bibliography | 161

Introduction

Although the fig tree shall not blossom, neither shall fruit be in the vines; the labour of the olive shall fail, and the fields shall yield no meat; the flock shall be cut off from the fold, and there shall be no herd in the stalls: Yet I will rejoice in the Lord, I will joy in the God of my salvation. The Lord God is my strength, and he will make my feet like hinds' feet, and he will make me to walk upon mine high places (Hab 3:17–19).

HABAKKUK WAS A PROPHET who foresaw the demise of his nation. While all around him signaled willful alienation from God, he wrote these lines of beauty and joy. For he knew that a person's state is determined, not by outward circumstance but by the imperturbable Light of Christ, given and received within.

Composed mostly over the last decade, the essays in this book record insights into the faith given me. Many of the themes began with inward promptings that arose from day-to-day interactions with others, with my surroundings, or with Scripture. Some inkling of Truth would begin to stir in my soul, and I would feel its momentum gather until a sense of urgency compelled me to give it a form that would communicate its validity to others. To bring meaning and beauty into being through the use of words is what I love to do, and trusting the Truth to guide and monitor my expression is pure delight.

Though I've studied the New Testament and early Friends' writings for nearly four decades, I have never sought to imitate or repeat their ideas in a secondhand manner, for each age must speak its own knowledge of God in its particular voice. If authentic, the testimonies from every time and place will show—to the enlightened mind—a unity of Spirit. Though not

Introduction

allowing the letter of Scriptures or early Friends' writings to displace the prerogative of Spirit, I have often cited these sources. Using the King James Version unless otherwise noted, I've quoted both Scriptures and Friends to support my assertions with their good sense and authority. Additionally, the reference to these earlier writings demonstrates the coherence of the faith from century to century, from millennium to millennium. Augustine refers to this continuum when he writes:

> That which is now called the Christian religion existed among the ancients, and never did not exist from the planting of the human race until Christ came in the flesh, at which time the true religion which already existed began to be called Christianity.[1]

May these essays be received as a present-day witness to the same faith that was held by early Friends and put forth by the prophets and apostles as recorded in Scripture. May they be so to those living now, and to those who will come after, that they might see the continuity through time of "that which is eternal, which gathers your hearts together up to the Lord, and lets you see that ye are written in one another's hearts."[2]

July 2021
Philadelphia, Pa.

---

1. Strong, *Scattered Brotherhood*, 3.
2. Fox, *Works*, 7:31.

A Colony of Heaven

In December 2018, in his blog *Can you believe?* Johan Maurer offered an opportunity to voice one's thoughts on what constitutes a faith community through taking a survey he'd composed titled "Building a Trustworthy Church." In this survey, participants were asked to describe their experience of trustworthiness (or its lack) in religious communities they'd been part of, and also to rate the importance of particular qualities or features for sustaining a trustworthy religious community. The survey included questions on the nature of leadership, culture, education, and finance.

Participants were also asked to envision "qualities or features [that] would be most important to include in any congregation [they] might consider joining." As I began to write my response to this particular question, I found more and more ideas tumbling forward, and upon completing my answer, noticed myself re-visiting the long-ago feeling of being six years old and having finished my Christmas list! Here's my list of the features and qualities:

> The primary feature would be a genuine knowledge of God and Christ. I'd want to see some effort had been given to studying Scripture and early Friends writings, additionally contemporary writers who have studied these original resources and written sensibly about their findings. I'd want to see good character, not only in major issues such as marital fidelity but in minor day-to-day behaviors, such as not monopolizing conversations or podium time, etc. In short, I'd want to see some self-awareness and discipline counteracting the fallen nature's tendency to self-aggrandizement. I'd like to see a creative, personal approach to worship and socializing: the house church where each brings a psalm or prayer and worshipers gather around a table to share and joyfully have a meal together sounds like an ideal. I'd like to see true friendliness and concern about one another's lives. I'd like to feel that the group was

truly the body of Christ, a colony of heaven. I'd like to hear others minister the Word of God.[1]

There is in every culture a germ or seed of origin that determines its form and function. In time, too many accretions burden the entity; distort its function; and cause it to fail, to die, leaving behind a hollow shell of what once lived. Prophets call us to honor and return to the source, the living seed, and not to worship the cultural casing that once held its outgrowth. George Fox here recalls the small beginning of the church in apostles' time when they said:

> "[P]ray every where"; who met together in their several houses, and went from house to house. Acts 2. 46. And this was the practice of the church in the primitive times, which we observe, who were to edify one another, and exhort one another, and build up one another, and pray for one another, and they were not to be tied to one place, synagogue, or temple, which the Jews were only, but sometimes they met on mountains and hills, and sometimes in houses. And the church was in Aquila and Priscilla's house, 1 Cor 16:19; there was a meeting set up in the primitive time.[2]

---

1. Maurer, "Trustworthy Church."
2. Fox, *Works*, 4:269.

Questionnaire

In November 2019, I received an email from Sergio de Moura, an adjunct professor at a university named UNILAB, which is located in Redenção, Brazil. Sergio informed me that although Brazil has more than 200 million inhabitants, the country has no Friends meeting. Having long considered becoming a Quaker himself, he wanted to publish writing from a Quaker perspective for others in his country who were likewise interested in the faith, and so was requesting permission to translate my essays into Portuguese and to publish them. Though he was particularly interested in the Quaker way of worship, he also asked if I would answer some general questions about Friends faith and life in a questionnaire that he intended to send out to a number of Friends from different areas. The following is a copy of the completed questionnaire that I returned to him.

1. *How have the Quakers' teachings influenced your life? When did this journey start?*

   I first became interested in spiritual matters in my early teens and would discuss ideas with my grandfather and also with friends. I began to read about various world religions at this time, and a few years later, began reading philosophy and literature that addressed spiritual questions. I continued to follow this interest in college where I studied literature. Throughout this entire time, my heart was heavy because I had no certain understanding of truth that could provide a foundation for my life, and so I felt ungrounded and lacked confidence and hope. I identified as an agnostic and felt no interest in or drawing to religious practice or belief. I became deeply depressed in my late 20s and remained near despair until age 32, when a specific, powerful revelation of eternal Being was given to me. Though inwardly changed from that time, I began to seek religious affiliation only a year and a half later. (I believe I needed time to accustom myself to this new way of being before taking any outward action.) I then found the Religious Society of Friends (Quakers) and began attending meetings each week, and began to read Isaac Penington and later George Fox, both seventeenth-century Friends. Both men's writings powerfully expressed my experience and understanding, as revealed in that initial epiphany and thereafter in worship. I became very active in the spiritual work of Philadelphia Yearly Meeting (the Quaker organization in this geographic area) at the local and regional levels and continued this work for a decade and a half. During that time, I became convinced Liberal Quakers (whom the yearly meeting comprised by and large) had little understanding of or interest in the original Quaker mission and message, and I withdrew my membership. In the past decade, I've continued my work as an essay writer[1] and take opportunities to share fellowship with those who fear God and are committed to the Truth.

2. *"To have a relationship with Jesus" is a notion so widespread by many Evangelicals, so much present in their religious culture and deeply rooted in their theology. As a Quaker, how do you see this idea? Does it work in a Quaker setting or how far do Friends agree or disagree with this conception?*

My understanding of Evangelical Christianity is that it differs theologically from the faith of seventeenth-century Friends, the faith that I affirm. A shorthand distinction is this: Evangelicals identify their faith with the affirmation that Jesus Christ is their personal Lord and Savior: they choose to accept Jesus. The Friends of the seventeenth century did not choose to accept Jesus; Jesus chose to accept them.[2] In other words, faith is not an act of will but a gift from God (Rom 9:16). Friends derived their name from the verse preceding the one aforementioned, i.e., John 15:15:

> Henceforth I call you not servants; for the servant knoweth not what his lord doeth: but I have called you friends; for all things that I have heard of my Father I have made known unto you.

This verse centers upon the choice of Jesus to make himself, the Word of God, known to us: that he does so is the "continuing revelation" that is the primary Quaker distinctive.

---

1. Dallmann, *Abiding Quaker* (blog).
2. John 15:16 (King James Version; all subsequent citations are from this version).

Questionnaire

3. *About "the light within" and "that of God in everyone," how do these concepts work for Friends and specially for you?*

The light within is experienced inwardly; it purifies and sanctifies my being. It is what I seek, expect, and hope for as I sit in silence; it informs my conscience, making me better able to live in a way that sees and thus glorifies God. Knowing its availability, I can act with strength and virtue, even when my natural inclination would have me do otherwise. It avails me of peace, order, joy, and every goodness I could want; it is the pearl of great price. As for the other phrase you've chosen (that of God in everyone), I caution you that this phrase has been taken by Liberal Friends from Fox's writing and used in a way Fox did not intend nor would agree with: Liberal Friends use the phrase to mean that which is virtuous and of value to the first-birth nature. There is no room in Liberal understanding for the second birth, which Jesus tells Nicodemus (John 3:3) must occur.

4. *Do you think of Friends as an "exclusive group" or as taking part in a "selective club"? I ask this considering that when compared to other Christian or not Christian groups, Quakers represent a very little spark of the religious culture. I mean, they are a reduced small group.*

Did Jesus see those who understood his teaching to be an "exclusive group" or "selective club"? No, he did not; however, he did say: "Because strait is the gate, and narrow is the way, which leadeth unto life, and few there be that find it" (Matt 7:14).

(a) A lot of people out and faraway of the Quaker mainstream centers are eager for that kind of comprehension about the light within, while Quakers seem to have decided "to hide themselves" from the world.

It is the concern of like-minded Friends that people who are far from Quaker centers are not likely to hear of the Quaker faith. We are hopeful that the technical advances in communication that have taken place in recent decades will enable more of these people to discover the existence of this precious faith that is being practiced among us, and they will get in touch.

(b) It seems that a culture of secularization reached many religious settings, including Quakers. It implies perhaps that there has been a loss of interest for spirituality, and it has reduced the numbers of adherents in Christian meetings.

I have found secularization to have taken place in Liberal meetings, and for this reason I withdrew. The Liberals' culture is secular in that social justice issues are given attention, and Christ is not known or heard. In any religious group, the members often make an idol of the community and their acceptance within it. This has always been a problem, as can be seen in Jesus's dealings with those in his religious community: religious culture usurps the primacy of inward life, and this can be seen among Christian groups as well as among the Liberals.

> 5. *For some people, suffering and pain are proof that there is no God, once a good God shouldn't permit their creatures to suffer. How far the "light within" can help someone to deal with this assumption? What's your opinion about this affirmation?*

The book of Job examines and responds to the question of suffering by having God assert his wisdom in having ordered creation the way in which he did. The light within does give us understanding (wisdom) and acceptance of (and gratitude for!) the way creation is ordered, and we can glorify God for so ordering it, even though there is suffering. It is through holding to the truth while enduring suffering that we become prepared to receive the light of Christ within. We have Jesus's work on the Cross as an outward example of the inward work that we ourselves must undergo. This is the Quaker understanding of the cross: it is suffering for the Truth's sake. George Fox wrote:

> [T]he eternal God knows and his son Christ Jesus, it is for him alone and his truth's sake we suffer. . . . And so the Lord hath given us "not only to believe but also to suffer for his name and truth's sake"; and so it is the gift of God, with his eternal spirit and power, that doth uphold us in all our sufferings.[3]

The truth is we humans are limited, finite, mortal beings, and we do not have the power to prevent ourselves from undergoing loss of all kinds throughout our lives; to accept inwardly this truth is to die to any false notion of self.

> 6. *What is the Bible and the four Gospels for Quakers? Are they a light or do they just introduce the light to us? Would there have been a Quaker movement unless George Fox had had the insight of "the light within" right from the Gospel of John?*

---

3. Fox, *Works*, 8:251.

Questionnaire

Barclay's third proposition identifies the Scriptures as

> esteemed a *secondary rule, subordinate to the Spirit* [italics Barclay's] from which they have all their excellency and certainty; for as by the inward testimony of the Spirit we do alone truly know them, so they testify, that the Spirit is that guide by which the saints are led into all Truth: therefore, according to the Scriptures, the Spirit is the first and principal leader.[4]

Fox found that the Scriptures confirmed his inward experience of the Light Within:

> Yet I had no slight esteem of the Holy Scriptures, but they were very precious to me, for I was in that spirit by which they were given forth, and what the Lord opened in me I afterwards found was agreeable to them.[5]

7. *About Jesus:*

    (a) Did He die on the cross for our sins? Is he our savior?

    (b) Is he God, the Son of God or just a prophet?

The following quotation from Fox emphasizes the coming into unity with Christ, which is the one true atonement. Although Quakers held that Jesus "taste[d] death for every man" (Heb 2:9) on the Cross, they asserted none was redeemed but through the inward knowledge of and unity with Christ. Here's the quotation:

> Christ saith ... "No man can come to me, except the Father, which hath sent me, draw him" (John 6:44). Now what is the means by which God doth draw people to his Son, but by the Holy Spirit. ... God doth draw people from their unrighteousness and unholiness, to Christ, the righteous and holy One, the great Prophet, in his New Covenant and New Testament, whom Moses in the Old Covenant and Old Testament said, God would raise up, like unto him, and whom people should "hear in all things." ... They that do not hear the Son of God, the great Prophet, do not mind the drawing of the Father by his Holy Spirit to his Son; but to them that mind the drawings of the good Spirit of the Father to his Son, the Spirit giveth understanding to know God and Jesus Christ. ... Then they know that Jesus Christ is the way ... and that none can

---

4. Barclay, *Apology*, 11.
5. Nickalls, *Journal*, 34.

come unto God but by and through his Son . . . they know that Christ is their Mediator and . . . their High-priest . . . and is able to the utmost to save all that come to God by him.[6]

---

6. Benson, *Notes*, SP7.

Each Gives Out of His Store

My first book on religion came from my grandparents the Christmas I was fourteen. Its title was *What the Great Religions Believe* by author Joseph Gaer. Deep discussions with my grandfather occurred almost every night in those early teenage years, while he washed and I dried the dishes after dinner. Religion was a topic that interested us both, and I'm grateful that I can recall some of his wisdom.

My views were very different then: I was becoming surer of my agnosticism with each month that passed, a perspective that was to last for most of the next two decades. Part of his wisdom was accepting my fourteen-year-old ideas as worthy of discussion. My views now are no doubt closer to what his were then, as is my age.

I was reminded recently of one vignette in this book, and thought I'd share it here. It is one of a number of unauthenticated sayings of Jesus that were found in papyri in Upper Egypt in the late-nineteenth century and were thought to have been written between 150 and 300 AD. The sayings, or Agrapha, were written in Greek. So, here's the story:

> One day Jesus and his disciples passed a man who spoke evil of them in a loud voice; but Jesus spoke only good in return. And when his disciples asked him why he spoke good to him who spoke evil, he replied: "Each gives out of his store."[1]

I'd like to think that my grandfather and I talked about that story.

---

1. Gaer, *Great Religions*, 141.

Partaking of the Sufferings

And our hope of you is stedfast, knowing, that as ye are partakers of the sufferings, so shall ye be also of the consolation (2 Cor 1:7).

IN A WORLD THAT is ever plagued by deceit and cruelty, suffering seems unavoidable. Yet Paul in this verse implies that suffering is optional: one may choose to partake of the sufferings or refuse to partake; one may accept or reject suffering. How is it possible to refuse to suffer when loss, injury, abuse, and death come to everyone? Not only does Paul advocate partaking of the sufferings, he makes being "of the consolation" contingent upon it. Assuming Paul is correct that salvation follows a partaking of suffering and this partaking is not automatic but must be chosen, the meaning of the phrase "partakers of the sufferings" is worth looking into.

A feeling of diminishment, whether from loss or the fear of loss, comes into every life, and we are free to respond in any number of ways. Paul advocates for a particular handling of these feelings, in such a way that we are prepared to receive the consolation of Christ, and he also implies that a contrary approach does not lead to receiving Christ. Examples of each will illustrate the difference between the two, and so, I will present the approach of first-generation Friends by looking at some passages from George Fox's journal that document his early years. Before doing so, however, I'll present a diametrically opposed approach to that of the first Friends. This contrasting ethos is embodied in Roman Carnival revelers of the nineteenth century. Though these two approaches differ, the challenge that each group faced was the same and is, in fact, universal.

It was once a custom among the inhabitants of Rome to celebrate Carnival in the time before Lent. The word "Carnival" is drawn from its Latin root *carnem levare* and means "remove the meat." The Latin root has also given us the word "carnal," which is used in Scripture to signify that which is not spiritual: "fleshly" and "worldly" being synonyms. The distinction is made clear by Fox in the following passage in which he refers to Paul's use of the word "carnal":

> If they be not carnal, then they are spiritual . . . things seen . . . are temporal and carnal; and what is temporal is not eternal, nor spirit. The apostle speaks of "carnal weapons," 2 Cor 10:4, and "carnal ordinances" Heb 9:10.[1]

Carnival was a time of self-indulgent and thoughtless behavior, a time of personal display, extravagance, masquerades, contests, and parties. On the final night of Carnival, Romans crowded into the main thoroughfare of their city to play a game called "Moccoletti" in which each celebrant lit and carried a candle. The goal of Moccoletti was to extinguish another's flame while keeping one's own burning. Any ploy, subterfuge, or fraud was to be expected in this contest, as there were no rules. Charles Dickens in *Pictures from Italy* describes the scene:

> Then everybody present has but one engrossing object, that is, to extinguish other people's candles and to keep his own alight; and everybody: man, woman, or child, gentleman or lady, prince or peasant, native or foreigner yells and screams, and roars incessantly, as a taunt to the subdued, "Senza Moccolo, Senza Moccolo!" (Without a light! Without a light!) until nothing is heard but a gigantic chorus of those two words, mingled with peals of laughter.[2]

At midnight with the ringing of church bells throughout the city, Moccoletti was over; Carnival was finished and Lent began. At that moment, the highest contrast in behavior could be observed: the frenzy of Moccoletti vanished into the somber season of Lent. Dickens describes the abrupt changeover in this way:

> When in the wildest enthusiasm of the cry, and fullest ecstasy of the sport, the Ave Maria rings from the church steeples, and the Carnival is over in an instant—put out like a taper with a breath![3]

Since first learning many years ago of this Roman Carnival practice, I have thought of it as a metaphor for the spiritually darkened, routine

---

1. *Epigraph*. 2 Cor 1:7 (King James Version [KJV]). Fox, *Works*, 3:78.
2. Dickens, *Italy*, 127.
3. Dickens, *Italy*, 128.

happenings in our world that result from a prevailing "carnal" or worldly approach to being alive; and conversely, Lent, which immediately follows Carnival, as its antithesis. Lent occurs in the forty days preceding Easter and is a time of socially enforced asceticism, in which participants refrain from self-indulgence, reflect upon their misdeeds, and thus come to feel a heightened sense of personal emptiness, absence, and need. It is a time of penitence, of thoughtful self-scrutiny. That the two seasons of Carnival and Lent abut is no accident; the stark difference between their respective worldviews is accentuated by their proximity: the natural, mundane life followed by a disciplined restraint that would prepare for some new and better way of life, a way yet unknown to either the carnal-minded or the ascetic.

Two centuries before Dickens wrote about the Roman Carnival, the seventeenth-century men and women that would bring forth the Quaker movement had been engaged in something like a Lenten practice. George Fox and others subjected themselves to rigorous self-examination that was, in fact, the awareness the Lenten discipline was intended to evoke. That Friends opted to undergo this self-scrutiny in the absence of any cultural prod vouches for their having been guided not by a culturally religious prescription but by "the light of [their] nature," as Paul describes some Gentiles in the book of Romans:

> When Gentiles who do not possess the law carry out its precepts by the light of nature, then . . . they are their own law, for they display the effect of the law inscribed on their hearts. Their conscience is called as witness, and their own thoughts argue the case on either side, against them or even for them, on the day when God judges the secrets of human hearts through Christ Jesus.[4]

Both the Gentiles that Paul refers to in these verses and the early Quakers subjected themselves to the dictate of the pure law of God:

> . . . the light in the conscience before faith. And the law is the light and the schoolmaster until faith . . . men have this light before they believe in it, and are children . . . then afterwards to believe in it; and with it they see the author of their faith, Christ Jesus, from whom it comes.[5]

---

4. Rom 2:14–16 (The New English Bible [NEB]).
5. Fox, *Works*, 3:68.

This standard of righteousness (the law, the light in the conscience, the schoolmaster) when attended to and learned from does ensure that all that must happen, will happen:

> Do not suppose that I have come to abolish the Law and the prophets; I did not come to abolish, but to complete. I tell you this: so long as heaven and earth endure, not a letter, not a stroke, will disappear from the Law until all that must happen has happened (Matt 5:17–18 [NEB]).

In the first few pages of George Fox's journal, we learn of his attention to righteous behavior. Before he had received faith from Christ, he diligently attended to the Light in his conscience, the schoolmaster. He speaks of his early memories of feeling offended at seeing "old men carry themselves lightly and wantonly towards each other"[6] and of his aversion to "foul ways and devouring the creation":

> But people being strangers to the covenant of life with God, they eat and drink to make themselves wanton with the creatures, devouring them upon their own lusts, and living in all filthiness, loving foul ways and devouring the creation; and all this in the world, in the pollutions thereof, without God; and therefore I was to shun all such.[7]

Unlike the Roman populace, Fox felt repulsed by self-indulgent, corrupt behavior, and instead was drawn to behaving in a way that is in "unity with the creation." Those who attended to the light in their consciences were, says Paul, "their own law." Within themselves, there would be an honest struggle to discover and live by what was right, even if it required inner conflict: "their own thoughts argue the case on either side against or even for them." Fox engaged in such conscientious self-questioning and argument, as here is shown:

> And I wondered why these things should come to me. . . . Then I thought, because I had forsaken my relations I had done amiss against them; so I was brought to call to mind all my time that I had spent and to consider whether I had wronged any. . . . I was about twenty years of age when these exercises came upon me, and

---

6. Nickalls, *Journal*, 1.
7. Nickalls, *Journal*, 2.

> some years I continued in that condition, in great trouble; and fain I would have put it from me.[8]

He "would have put it from [him]" because his self-questioning was troublesome, painful to the point of despair. Yet he willingly endured this painful uncertainty about himself; he willingly partook of these sufferings, because he could accept no false solution or relief from them: no provisional cultural, social, intellectually speculative, or theological answer could suffice for him: he honored the truth and endured the cost. Neither able to deny his inner reality nor to anticipate any resolution, Fox simply partook of the suffering: "I cannot declare the misery I was in, it was so great and heavy upon me."[9] Unlike most, he endured this severe tension without resorting to hypocrisy, aggression, legalism, conformity, or dissipation. He partook of the suffering that accompanies knowing oneself to be in existential need with no real solution in sight: in truth, he felt and saw himself as he was—without God.

Fox's misery departed after he had been given faith, immediate knowledge of God and Jesus Christ whom he had sent. At ease in God's love, Fox could now view himself with equanimity [italics mine]:

> Then the Lord gently led me along, and let me see his love, which was endless and eternal, surpassing all the knowledge that men have in the natural state, or can get by history or books. *That love let me see myself, as I was without him*; and I was afraid of all company: for I saw them perfectly, where they were, through the love of God which let me see myself.[10]

Receiving faith through hearing Christ, the Word of God, was the life-changing event for Fox, and so it is for everyone who follows the same excruciating path of partaking of sufferings. Receiving faith ends the old, worldly order of misery as well as the moral evil that arises from humanity's determination to muffle and quell the fear of weakness and self-diminishment, the fear of death.

Emil Brunner in *The Christian Doctrine of Church, Faith, and the Consummation* outlines the inevitable progression from fear of death to wickedness:

---

8. Nickalls, *Journal*, 4.
9. Nickalls, *Journal*, 10.
10. Fox, *Works*, 1:74.

Between death and moral evil there is from the standpoint of experience a scarcely comprehensible, but none the less real, relation. Moral evil, in so far as it is not pure defiance but also weakness, is rooted in anxiety, and this anxiety is in the last resort always the fear of death. All insatiable hunger for power, all the cruelty of tyrants, all the timidity of the narrow-minded—what are they but attempts to find security from an unknown threat? Our wickedness—human wickedness—is not so much . . . a defiant "No" to the Creator's will as the expression of a latent panic in the face of coming death. Fear of death is the secret cause of moral evil, as death itself is moral evil's manifest result: "the wages of sin."[11]

Glancing backward to the Roman revelers, we see the crowd pressing each person into keeping a vigilant eye focused outward: One's stealthy neighbor might put out one's flame! How humiliating and diminishing that would be! Like a symbolic death! Better to put out another's flame first! thinks each anxiety-filled reveler.

What abundant conflict is entailed in this routine aggressive/defensive behavior! And what diversion! The conflict—playful here but serious in society, and deadly serious among ethnically diverse societies—keeps people busy and avoiding the hard work of looking within, and each seeing himself as he is. One might occupy oneself indefinitely brandishing and thwarting power for term of life! One might never move beyond this state of sin in which fear of death, and thus death itself has its reign.

If in place of the lit candle of Roman Moccoletti, we substitute rights, property, status, influence, opportunity, dignity, or physical life itself, the senseless conflict in the world arising from fraud, abuse, violence, and war is seen for what it fundamentally is: an outward distraction that enables and promotes the refusal to suffer honest self-scrutiny that is, in truth, the obligation of each human being to undergo. For it is undergoing self-scrutiny that a person prepares himself to receive God's gift of grace and life.

Fearful defense of natural assets is just as surely an outward diversion as is the aggressive acquiring of them; therefore, are we told: "If a man wants to sue you for your shirt, let him have your coat as well" (Matt 5:40 [NEB]). All the aggression and defensiveness denies and masks the naked truth that we each in our human nature are not complete, not whole, not absolute, not total, not immortal. Shameful as that feels, we need to partake of that knowledge: the revealing of the self that does not know God, and

---

11. Brunner, *Doctrine of the Church*, 437.

instead lawlessly attempts to usurp his place by claiming our natural being is whole, absolute, independent, autonomous, and in charge.

The problem for the person of sin is a lawless, false self-projection arising from a terror of truth that can be revealed at any moment. In the day of visitation, however, all is revealed:

> for that day shall not come, except there come a falling away first, and that man of sin be revealed, the son of perdition; Who opposeth and exalteth himself above all that is called God, or that is worshipped; so that he as God sitteth in the temple of God, shewing himself that he is God (2 Thess 2:3b–4 [KJV]).

Though it's not always Carnival season in the mid-1800s, the carnal mind sets itself in the aggressive/defensive posture that is found in the Carnival game, often without an awareness of having done so. For example, many Quakers presume their calling to be working to eliminate social ills that beleaguer our world, and accordingly have focused their attention outward to extend or defend contemporary Quaker values that are referred to as the testimonies. A rationale of improving social conditions through championing causes provides ample assignment to occupy time and consciousness, and this activity substitutes human aspiration to virtue for knowledge of and a hearing/obeying response to God.

Neither entertaining diversion nor a focus on social justice work honors or manifests the faith found by Fox and other early Quakers who braved examining their souls in the light of the standard of Truth, the divine law. Instead, people refuse to endure the inward scrutiny that reveals the failure of usurped autonomy. Again from *The Christian Doctrine of Church, Faith, and the Consummation,* Brunner shows the correlation of this false claim to independence and a life given over to death:

> When man as a sinner denies his dependence on God and turns it into independence, he is severed from God, the original source of all life; his guilt stands between the living God and himself as he actually is. Thus the creature destroys the root of its own life, its fellowship with God. But man is unable utterly to destroy the relation to God which was established by God the Creator. He remains bound to God, but now instead of living in the love of God, he is under God's wrath. . . . The shadow of judgment lies upon his whole life and makes it a life in darkness, in exile. This life in its totality is in fact a "being unto death."[12]

---

12. Brunner, *Doctrine of the Church,* 386–87.

Partaking of the Sufferings

William Stringfellow in his *An Ethic for Christians & Other Aliens in a Strange Land* identifies all nations, all institutions as embodying a demonic idolatry of death. He argues that a fear and worship of death is the attempt to furnish meaning but results in social chaos in many forms: racism, ecological corruption, misogyny, conformity, violence, etc. This situation can't be eradicated, he claims, but he does offer guidance on how to live humanly in the midst of it: resistance to the power of death and a "biblical style of life." The following excerpt from Stringfellow on resisting the power of death would certainly have been agreed to by Fox:

> In the face of death, live humanly. In the middle of chaos, celebrate the Word. Amidst babel, I repeat, speak the truth. Confront the noise and verbiage and falsehood of death with the truth and potency and efficacy of the Word of God. Know the Word, teach the Word, nurture the Word, preach the Word, defend the Word, incarnate the Word, do the Word, live the Word. And more than that, in the Word of God, expose death and all death's works and wiles, rebuke lies, cast out demons, exorcise, cleanse the possessed, raise those who are dead in mind and conscience.[13]

It is through a humble willingness to endure the truth of ourselves, even unto the brokenness that is typified by death on the cross, that we become prepared. This partaking of the sufferings, we discover, is followed by the Lord's coming to dwell with us, a resurrection to unforeseen, abundant life. No longer do we depend on the powers of nature to vivify and secure ourselves; no longer do we fear the loss of our natural powers, for, as the prophet Isaiah proclaims, the Lord shall be our everlasting light, and the days of mourning shall be ended.

> The sun shall be no more thy light by day; neither for brightness shall the moon give light unto thee: but the LORD shall be unto thee an everlasting light, and thy God thy glory. Thy sun shall no more go down; neither shall thy moon withdraw itself: for the Lord shall be thine everlasting light, and the days of thy mourning shall be ended (Isa 60:19–20 [KJV]).

---

13. Stringfellow, *Ethic for Christians*, 142–43.

The Ubiquitous War of the Lamb

Man is the land where . . . two kings fight; and whatever is good and holy belongs to the one king, and whatever is evil and unclean belongs to the other; and there is no communion or peace between them. . . . And where the fight is once begun between these, there is no quietness in that land, till one of these be dispossessed: but then there is either the peace of Babylon, most commonly under a form of holiness; or the peace of Sion, in the spirit, life, and power.
—Isaac Penington

A FEW YEARS AGO, I was regularly attending worship at a meeting in Philadelphia. For some years, I went to this particular meeting because it was the only meeting I knew that still had several members with old Quaker surnames, and thus, there was still in evidence something approximating old Quaker theology.

As is typical in meetings, week after week Friends would settle into worship, each on a particular bench that had unobtrusively gained acceptance by all as that person's domain, their perch year after year, and for a family, generation after generation. I—having been a Quaker for but a few decades—shared a bench with a longtime Friend (or he shared his bench with me) for a couple of years, during which time he informed me that this bench had been his family's for more than a century.

This Friend was a neuroscientist, and though he had the old Quaker surname (and the bench), he did not have the old Quaker understanding. He was a positivist; and one of the ways he showed his stripes was by evaluating all ministry given during the hour using the sole criterion of time: the ministry was either the right length or it was too long. At the close of each meeting, he would—according to this standard—offer me his evaluation of the ministry (the ministry of others or of myself, if I'd ministered). Seeing his constancy in this practice, I gently expressed my amusement and let him know that there could be other standards to consider when evaluating vocal ministry.

There were, however, other discrepancies in understanding between him and me. In the occasional post-meeting discussion on some spiritual topic, we each would find the other's perspective in need of further consideration . . . further consideration by the other. Following a number of disagreements over the months, I began to sense there could be no common spiritual ground between a positivist and a Christian. This slow-footed clarity arrived one Sunday morning following a particularly rigorous discussion after meeting for worship.

The exchange culminated while we stood near an open door of the by then empty meetinghouse. Over six-feet tall, the man towered above. Lowering and wagging his finger inches from my nose, he yelled, "There is no God! You have to stop believing that!"

More problematic than the man's stated atheism was his shouted command: "You have to stop believing that!"

Some might claim that George Fox and other early Friends—perhaps this fellow's ancestors—could be equally vehement when speaking for their belief, but that would miss the point. It was this man's *manner of persuasion* that was foreign to and had no place in early Friends' practice. Convincement occurred when Friends preached the gospel. "[T]hat which may be known of God"[1] was evoked, and often their hearers were inwardly transformed. A new sense of life, of dignity, power, and responsibility was known when "the life [that] was the light of men" (John 1:4) appeared within. The soul at last knew its worth; the person was edified: he or she had become inwardly established.

In contrast, this positivist's hope rested upon closing down another's inward life: closing down the high human capacity for discernment and discovery, thus reducing a human being to something less than a person. His sole "convincing" power was a fiat delivered with a tone and gesture of violence, a tactic of depersonalization.

Unbeknownst to him or to me that morning, we each embodied a force that in relation to the other, as Penington wrote, had "no communion or peace between them"; these forces contend (like the two kings referred to

---

1 *Epigraph.* Penington, *Works*, 1:141. Rom 1:19 (King James Version; all subsequent citations are from this version).

in the epigraph) for the soul of humanity: to edify or to destroy. Though this Sunday morning incident involved only two people in an empty meetinghouse, it was, nevertheless, the Lamb's War: a skirmish in which the powers clashed, powers which when pitted against one another on a grander scale determine history.

In *Christianity and Civilisation*, originally presented as Gifford Lectures (1947–1948), Emil Brunner, a Reformed theologian of the mid-twentieth century, summarizes the devolution of a civilization that is based upon the Judeo-Christian understanding that man is created in the image of God (Gen 1:27). Our civilization was transformed slowly, beginning with the Enlightenment and taking several centuries. Here Brunner gives a short history of the long travel from faith to fascism:

> At first, the alternative to the Christian idea was still a religious although no longer distinctly Christian theism. Then further from the Christian foundation, there came a transcendentalism or idealism, which still remained metaphysical although no longer explicitly theistic. In the middle of the last century this idealistic humanism was replaced by a positivist philosophy of freedom and civilization, which acknowledged no metaphysical but merely natural presuppositions. It is not surprising that this positivism, in its turn more and more, lost its humanistic contents and turned into a naturalistic philosophy for which man was no more than a highly developed animal, the cerebral animal, and this was a conception of man within which such things as the dignity of man, the rights of man, and personality no longer had any foundation.[2]

Being Swiss, Brunner saw close at hand the outcome of centuries of anti-spiritual forces at work, as countries encircling his own fell into totalitarianism in the 1930s. Those bastard political systems—Fascism and National Socialism—were born and bore the marks of their spiritual progenitor, whose countenance was eventually recognized as nihilism. Brunner continues:

> Benjamin Constant, that noble Christian philosopher of freedom of the early nineteenth century, has comprehended the essence of this whole process of modern history in three words: "De la divinité par l'humanité à la bestialité" [from Divinity by humanity to bestiality]. The totalitarian revolutions with their practice of inhumanity, lawlessness, and depersonalizing collectivism were nothing but the executors of this so-called positivist philosophy, which as a

---

2. Brunner, *Civilisation*, 3.

matter of fact was a latent nihilism and which, towards the end of the last and the beginning of this century, had become the ruling philosophy of our universities and the dominating factor within the worldview of the educated and the leading strata of society.[3] [Italics are mine.]

In Brunner's summary, which ties forms of political order to the Zeitgeist, or spiritual condition of the age, we note that our own nation was begun at a propitious time. Our founders were eighteenth-century people of the Enlightenment, proponents of reason, who enjoyed the benefits that had accrued from a Christian civilization with its doctrine of man having been made in God's image, and therefore deserving of dignity. This worldview had so long prevailed that the idea of man's inalienable rights could be "truths [held] to be self-evident," and as such, individual rights were engrafted into our Constitution, and the rule of law upheld in recognizing that document's authority.

Without the undergirding Christian worldview, civil rights are not self-evident. With the loss of Christianity and the Enlightenment's residual cultural assumptions, our social order is threatened. Its continuity rests upon links thin and attenuated, ready to snap. Precedence, tradition, law, and the moral character of our government officials and citizenry are what now stand between us and brutal tyranny that commonly overtakes societies.

These past three years, our attention has been held by the drama of corruption, scandal, and deceit played out by the federal government's chief executive, and now we hear tyranny growling in the wings awaiting his cue to pounce onto center stage. May the House managers succeed in ridding us of this bad actor who has undertaken an unprecedented assault upon our Constitution, our nation's long adhered to script of civic rights and order. We take heart in legislators' determination to present evidence and argue soundly against the travesty of Trump remaining in office.

From New York representative Jerrold Nadler comes this January 24, 2020, statement before the Senate:

> President Trump is an outlier. He is the first and only President ever to declare himself unaccountable and to ignore subpoenas backed by the Constitution's impeachment power. If he is not removed from office, if he is permitted to defy the Congress entirely, categorically, to say subpoenas from Congress in the impeachment

---

3. Brunner, *Civilisation*, 3.

inquiry are nonsense, then we will have lost (the House will have lost, and certainly the Senate will have lost) all power to hold any President accountable. This is a determination by President Trump that he wants to be all powerful; he does not have to respect the Congress; he does not have to respect the representatives of the people; only his will goes. He is a dictator. This must not stand. And this is another reason he must be removed from office.[4]

---

4. *WSJ* editorial board, "Dictator."

Doing Our Part

In August 2015, I wrote an essay titled "The Only Antidote," in which I argued for the need to think critically: to use natural powers of reason and conscience to honor, discern, and communicate the truth. Referring to Hannah Arendt's understanding of the cause behind the rise of Fascism and also referring to a Bible story of John the Baptist's execution by Herod, I pointed to the crucial and perennial role of critical thought in containing the spread of evil.

Although critical thought can check evil, I contended that ultimately it is no match. Nonetheless, the exercise of thinking critically benefits the soul immeasurably. In subjecting oneself to reason and conscience, we prepare the way of the Lord; decent, honest effort precedes the gift of faith that comes only from God. It is only through the power of God that evil can and will be overcome and destroyed, both within and without. "Repent for the Kingdom of God is at hand," say those who have known what's necessary and possible.

At the time I wrote that essay, our country was not in imminent danger of electing to its highest political office a man who sports an Orwellian disregard for truth. Now, however, in 2016, that threat looms: we the people of the United States might, in fact, elect to the presidency a man who represents, enables, and lauds speech and behavior that is beyond the pale of reason and conscience.

Stated at our country's founding was the claim that we are endowed by our Creator with "certain unalienable Rights." We have, in fact, been endowed by our Creator with certain inalienable responsibilities, that among them are right use of reason and conscience. Let's use them well.

If we assume that pervasive, severe moral catastrophe is not possible in our own country, we do well to heed those who have lived through complete breakdown in their own regions. In the following paragraph, Swiss theologian Emil Brunner, who witnessed firsthand Europe's descent into Fascism, traces the progression from idealistic humanist philosophy to tyrannical totalitarianism, inevitably occurring, says Brunner, when unchecked by a Christian tradition within that society:

> That is to say that idealistic humanism leads to an individualistic conception of society, which in the end must have anarchical consequences. That is why modern society in so far as it has relinquished its Christian basis appears to be in a state of latent anarchy or dissolution. With the middle of the nineteenth century, there begins a fierce reaction against this individualism, and this collectivist reaction in its turn is worked out logically from a naturalist philosophy. The alternative to idealistic individualism is not free communion but primitive tribal not to say animal collectivism. It is the de-personalized mass-man, the man forming a mere particle of a social structure and the centralized automatic mechanical totalitarian state, which inherits the decaying liberal democracy. Only where a strong Christian tradition had prevailed was it possible to avoid this fatal alternative of individualism and collectivism to preserve a federal non-centralized, pluralistic organic structure of the State, and therefore to avoid that sudden transition from a half anarchic individualism into a tyrannical totalitarianism. But the societies of the West, which abhor the way taken by totalitarian Russia, Italy, and Germany, do not yet seem to have grasped that if the process of de-Christianization goes on within their society, they too will inevitably go the same way.[1]

By the 1940s, the philosophy of idealism, against which Brunner warns, had begun in Quaker circles to displace the original prophetic, apostolic Christian faith of earlier centuries. This trend was recognized and revealed by Lewis Benson. In an excerpt from his essay "Prophetic Quakerism," Benson describes the difference between the two doctrines of the Inner Light: prophetic and philosophical:

> First, the *philosophical interpretation* understands the Inner Light to be that innate capacity of human beings to comprehend rational and ethical truth.... This view tends to make the concept of "spirit" in man identical with the concept of "mind."[2] [Italics are mine.]

---

1. Brunner, *Civilisation*, 101.
2. Benson, *Truth is Christ*, 14.

According to this view, the human psyche is by nature divine, as it is endowed with reason and a capacity for ethical consideration.

Distinct from this philosophical interpretation is the *prophetic doctrine* of the Inner Light, by which is understood, says Benson, "that man may become completely spiritualized, that is to say, brought into perfect harmony with the will of the Creator God who is spirit." This is not effected by man's natural ability but by divine "power which operates in man but which is nevertheless not of man . . . [that is to say] not present in man as his own psychological possession."[3]

The doctrines of "that of God in every one" and "the power of love and good will to overcome war and hate" are derived from the idealism that originates with the philosophical interpretation of the Inner Light. This doctrine is a tribute to human capacity and thus differs from the prophetic doctrine, which places man in total dependency on the power of God to inform his understanding of right and wrong, and to gather, govern, and preserve a people who have Christ as their head: "whose dominion and strength is over all, against whom," says Penington, "the gates of hell cannot prevail."[4]

Benson's piece, written in the middle of the Second World War, when civilization hung precariously in the balance, recognizes the limits of human ability and power to order and preserve the world and the necessity of coming into the knowledge of and obedience to the Will of God, as did the first Friends.

*

It is now October 2021; five years have passed since I wrote this essay shortly before Trump was elected. What has both heartened and dismayed me most during this treacherous time has been the repeated observation that one person can affect the well-being not only of a society but of the world.

We have had many heroes in the last five years. One after another, they have stepped forward to block the advance of tyranny by one who recognizes neither the legitimacy of law nor the sanctity of truth. Heroic men and women have done their part, and we are grateful beyond measure.

---

3. Benson, *Truth is Christ*, 14.
4. Penington, *Works*, 4:7.

Our eighteenth-century founders were wise about human nature; they "knew what was in man."[5] They saw that the progress and viability of our democracy depended largely upon the character of our leaders: that whoever occupied the office of President must be a person of high caliber.

In 1945, nearing the end of the Second World War, when President Franklin D. Roosevelt foresaw the new responsibility our country must assume within the community of nations, he affirmed the following words of President John Adams by having them carved into the mantle of the State dining room in the White House. The inscription is taken from a letter Adams wrote in 1800 to his wife, Abigail:

> I pray Heaven to bestow the best of blessings on this house and all that shall hereafter inhabit it. May none but honest and wise men ever rule under this roof.

May we thereafter add: "And all the people said, Amen" (1 Chron 16:36b).

---

5. John 2:25 (King James Version; all subsequent citations are from this version).

The Only Antidote

Because thou hast kept the word of my patience, I also will keep thee from the hour of temptation which shall come upon all the world, to try them that dwell upon the earth (Rev 3:10).

HANNAH ARENDT WAS A philosopher and political theorist who left Germany in the early 1930s. After having done relief work in France for some years, she was briefly held in a detention camp when France fell to the Nazis. She fled to the United States in 1941 where she taught and wrote for several decades. Some may be familiar with the phrase "the banality of evil" that she coined while covering the trial of war criminal Adolf Eichmann in Jerusalem in the early 1960s. It was Eichmann's "absence of thinking," Arendt wrote, "that awakened my interest. Is evil-doing . . . possible in default of not just 'base motives' . . . but of any motives whatsoever. . . . Might the problem of good and evil, our faculty of telling right from wrong, be connected with our faculty of thought?"[1]

Arendt came to believe that the great destruction wreaked during the times of Nazi and Stalinist totalitarianism was a direct result of the refusal to exercise our human capacity for critical thought. The forfeiture of reason opened the way for chaos and destruction, she claimed. The following is an excerpt from a monologue in the film titled *Hannah Arendt*:

> This inability to think created the possibility for many ordinary men to commit evil deeds on a gigantic scale, the like of which had never been seen before. The manifestation of the wind of thought is not knowledge but the ability to tell right from wrong, beautiful from ugly. And I hope that thinking gives people the strength to

---

1. *Epigraph.* Rev 3:10 (King James Version; all subsequent citations are from this version). Arendt, *Life of the Mind*.

prevent catastrophes in these rare moments when the chips are down.[2]

At another point in the film, Arendt defines radical evil as the continual obliteration of sense within daily surroundings that occurred in the concentration camps. Senselessness made superfluous the high mental functioning that distinguishes us as human beings. Thus, Arendt argued, the obliteration of sense was intended to make "human beings superfluous as human beings." In a classroom scene, she lectures her college students:

> Western tradition mistakenly assumes that the greatest evils of mankind arise from selfishness. But in our century, evil has proven to be more radical than was previously thought. And we now know that the truest evil, the radical evil, has nothing to do with selfishness or any such understandable sinful motives. Instead it is based on the following phenomenon: making human beings superfluous as human beings. The entire concentration camp system was designed to convince the prisoners they were unnecessary before they were murdered. In the concentration camps, men were taught that punishment was not connected to a crime, that exploitation wouldn't profit anyone, and that work produced no results. The camp is a place where every activity and human impulse is senseless: where, in other words, senselessness is daily produced anew.[3]

Later Arendt wrote in a personal letter that evil was "thought-defying," that its nothingness precipitated a frustration of thought. In that same letter, she modified her earlier view on radical evil.

> I changed my mind and do no longer speak of "radical evil.". . . It is indeed my opinion now that evil is never "radical," that it is only extreme, and that it possesses neither depth nor any demonic dimension. It can overgrow and lay waste the whole world precisely because it spreads like a fungus on the surface. It is "thought-defying," as I said because thought tries to reach some depth, to go to the roots, and the moment it concerns itself with evil, it is frustrated because there is nothing. That is its "banality." Only the good has depth and can be radical.[4]

---

2. von Trotta, *Hannah Arendt*.
3. von Trotta, *Hannah Arendt*.
4. Arendt, personal letter to Scholem, July 24, 1963.

Arendt thought that evil spreads when man forfeits his capacity to think deeply. She later concluded that thought is frustrated by evil, as "thought tries to reach some depth," and evil has no depth. She rightly saw that evil destroys man, and man cannot overcome it by his own power.

Arendt's ideas of the necessity for deep, critical thought to halt evil, and evil's impervious resistance to thought, has a scriptural corollary in the work and execution of John the Baptist. Like Arendt, John is calling people to engage in thought when he cries, "Repent ye: for the kingdom of heaven is at hand" (Matt 3:2). The word "repentance" at its etymological root means "to think differently." John's proclamation of the need for repentance is a call to begin to think more deeply and truthfully.

In the fourth chapters of both Matthew and Luke, John the Baptist's story surrounds the temptation story of Christ in the wilderness. Both John and Jesus spend time in the wilderness, for the wilderness is the place where independent thought occurs, apart from the city where group influence dominates. John prepares the way by calling people to begin to think more deeply, to think for themselves and not be conformed to the group: to repent of that. "Repent ye: for the kingdom of God is at hand," he urges (Matt 3:2). Furthermore, John acts with independence, clarity, and righteousness; he gives concise, righteous direction to people, publicans, and soldiers (Luke 3:10–14) who do not share his independence, his clarity. With clear resolve, he exhorts people, distinguishes right from wrong, the wheat from chaff (Luke 3:17), the worthwhile from the worthless.

Herod puts him in prison for it and beheads him. Herod's taking the head of John the Baptist symbolizes worldly power (Satan) eliminating the faculty of reason, intellect, mind. Arendt concluded that thought cannot overcome evil, and John's execution by Herod represents the same idea in a symbolic narrative.

Jesus, like John, will be executed by the world, with its love for power and glory that is Satan's to give. But unlike John, Jesus will overcome the power of death that Satan holds, for Jesus is "mightier" than John, as John informs those who receive his baptism (Matt 3:11). Following John's execution, Jesus takes up the ministry where John left off, echoing his very words: "Repent: for the kingdom of heaven is at hand" (Matt 4:17). Jesus, however, has undergone the wilderness temptation by Satan and, in keeping the word of the Father, has become established in right relationship with him. Therefore he, unlike John, is empowered to overcome the world, Satan, and death.

When Arendt claims that human thought cannot overcome evil, she is in accord with Scriptures, for John and the baptism with water that he ministers could not overcome evil. Thought is the purview of human beings. Though it is exceedingly important that we undertake this preparation of critical thought (that is, thinking differently, independently), thought itself is not sufficient: it is not the Way. Evil frustrates thought, as Arendt observed. Herod, symbol of the worldly power of Satan, kills John, the symbol of independent, righteous thought. A brief look at one of Satan's temptations shows how futile thought is when attempting to understand or overcome evil.

Satan's first temptation aimed at Jesus in the fourth chapter of Matthew employs a conditional if/then statement: "If thou be the Son of God, [then] command that these stones be made bread" (Matt 4:3). If/then statements are often used in arguments and show a causal relationship between two ideas: the form is a tool for determining truth or falsehood. Satan instead uses the if/then statement to obscure truth: he implies Jesus's Sonship is conditioned upon his successfully turning stone into bread. Additionally, when Satan says to Jesus "command these stones be made bread," he is issuing a command. For when Satan adjures a person to command, who actually commands: the person or Satan? The command is Satan's, and thus the person who follows Satan's command is subservient to him and is not, himself, in command. More, much more, could be said of the devil's tactics in this passage: how he would diminish and destroy; tempt Jesus to use his Sonship in service to self rather than God; how he would have Jesus to do away with himself, using Scripture as an authority to subvert. The confusion is rampant, and reason is frustrated and exhausted by attempting to untangle the lies of the devil, the father of lies (John 8:44).

The love of power and glory that entails willfully engaging in confusion and deceit is evil. When deceit and power are preferred to clarity and truth—darkness preferred to light—condemnation follows; humanity is lost. As human beings, we are called to love and strive for truth and understanding. Our love of truth that we can manifest in thoughtful exercise of reason and conscience (that is, in the different thinking called for by John the Baptist's call to repentance) is the necessary preparation to receive Christ, the Truth. In his essay, "Friends and the Truth," Lewis Benson affirms early Friends' devotion to truth.

> For early Friends truth was the ultimate value. George Fox says, "prize the truth above all things" and "love the truth more than

all." . . . Fox's conception of truth is grounded upon his belief that the life of man is determined by his relationship to his creator. . . . By listening to God and obeying his word man fulfills the basic law of his being. This basic conversational relationship between man and his creator is what Fox means by truth.[5]

If Man refuses to partake of this "dialogic relationship," his rightful position in relationship to God is lost. Benson continues: "This is the fall of man, the failure to hear and obey the creator . . . what Fox calls 'the fall from the truth.'"[6]

We're here today because we've gone through these trials; we've been tempted countless times to love something more than truth, and for the love of it, we've chosen truth instead, though our choice entails baptism into Christ's death, the world's brief triumph. We know that the eternal triumph, the resurrection to new life, follows the inward dying to the self. In that triumphant inward resurrection, we know not only rightness but the joy and the peace of having received Christ, the life, of having received the power to become sons of God. When we have known Christ, the Life, we are powerfully drawn to get the relationship with God right, to seek it with our whole heart. In the fourth chapters of Matthew and Luke, we see the elements of right relationship with God revealed by Jesus, who was led by the Holy Spirit into the wilderness, there to be tempted by the devil. Each of the three responses that Jesus gives holds one key element to that divine relationship that enables the human to surmount the core threat the devil poses: that is to say, the threat of separation from God, the loss of dialogic relationship.

Though appearing in different sequences, Satan's three temptations are the same in both the Matthew and Luke stories. Jesus's first response in each version describes what the human receives from God; in Matthew, the second response defines how the human is to enact his obligation to God; and the third response, what is his duty to God. (In Luke, the order is reversed for the second and third.) It is important for Jesus to affirm his understanding and partaking of the divine relationship prior to the start of his ministry, for he (as was John and every other prophet) is assaulted by the same power of Satan again and again during his work. The prophet's understanding and its source must be realized and available before he begins; that is his anointing to preach the gospel.

5. Benson, *Truth is Christ*, 55–56.
6. Benson, *Truth is Christ*, 56.

Jesus answers Satan's first challenge in the following statement: "It is written, Man shall not live by bread alone, but by every word that proceedeth out of the mouth of God" (Matt 4:4). Jesus implies that man is a spiritual being who cannot survive apart from the Spirit. Human sustenance is spiritual, the Word of God, not stones or bread, which are earthly. As human beings, Jesus says, we live "by every word that proceedeth out of the mouth of God." Satan intends to famish the human spirit by severing it from the provider of its true sustenance. Jesus rebuffs the temptation and articulates right understanding of what constitutes human life and what sustains it.

In the second temptation in Matthew, Satan suggests to Jesus that he cast himself down from the pinnacle of the temple; that if he believes the Scriptures, he should expect angels to prevent him from coming to harm. Jesus responds with these words: "It is written again, Thou shalt not tempt the Lord thy God" (4:7). Right relationship to God is again the issue in the second temptation. For man to assume that he knows what constitutes right action apart from God's command is usurpation. The devil tempts Jesus to take the initiative and to expect God to follow along. Conventional piety, ideals, speculation, doctrine are all typical ways man displaces the righteous hearing/obeying relationship with God. God is not tempted to follow along behind man's doctrines, principles, piety, and ideals to ensure that nothing goes amiss in man's determination to realize his ideations. No, ideals are no substitute for a hearing obedience to God; nothing humanly contrived is acceptable. The pious person falls into vanity when he fails to believe and accept Christ's admonition, "without me you can do nothing" (John 15:5b). Piety is a self-deception that one's own mind is an adequate substitute for God.

> And though a man may take up and perform something that is called religious, and pray with words, and read and talk of the Scriptures, and take up some cardinal outward ordinances, and in this content himself for a time; yet the witness of God's Holy Spirit shows him to be a hypocrite. He that seeks to cover and shelter himself while he lives in disobedience to the Spirit, seeking to be at ease in the flesh; this one will find that all is in vain, and there is no peace within, for the measure of God's Holy Spirit shows him that he still serves sin. Indeed, if a man should practice all those things which others have done by the Spirit and by the Life, and in which they formerly were accepted by God, yet this will not do, for God has no pleasure in this any more than if he "slays a man,

breaks a dog's neck, or offers swine's blood" (Isa 66:3). All this is abomination to the Lord.[7]

The third temptation that Jesus undergoes sums up the matter of right relationship with God in one defining statement: "Get thee hence, Satan: for it is written, Thou shalt worship the Lord thy God, and him only shalt thou serve" (Matt 4:10). Satan would entice by promising power and glory in exchange for subservience and worship. This is the stark choice: man worships God, or he worships the devil in his desire for worldly power and glory. The human obligation, states Jesus, is to worship and serve God only. This third and final response completes the description of right relationship between God and the Son of God.

From the start of our movement, Quakers held that we are to look inward while reading the Scriptures to find the truth of them in ourselves. We know that this Scripture passage of temptation in the wilderness refers not to Jesus alone but reveals the threat directed at our humanity to become less than human. We all regularly undergo this trial: to engage in deceit in exchange for power; our life depends upon our loving, prizing, and esteeming truth above worldly power and glory. The world will not love us for our choice, for we are not of it. Nevertheless, we can do no other than look to God, as Jesus did when tempted by the devil. For overcoming the world, death, and the devil can be done only through the power of God. Reason is insufficient to fathom or defeat evil. It is God's Word that sustains us in Life when we are tempted to confusion or deceit, and this is the substance of Jesus's retorts and example in the Scripture passage we examined. We receive sustaining life from God alone; we are not to usurp God's position of command by substituting our own human will; and we owe God our worship and service. We thank God that we have this passage to remind us of our rightful place and, more so, that we have the Light Within to guide us. The early Friends knew the strength of the enemy and heralded the only power great enough to overcome it. Christ's Light, wrote George Fox, is "the only antidote to overcome and expel the Poison of Satan's greatest Temptations."

> So if you mind the light, and in it stand, you will see the Lord giving issue, whereby you will find deliverance standing in the light, which comes from the word, which is a fire, and a hammer, and a sword, which beats down that which is contrary to the truth, divides and burns up, but keeping the word, the temptations will not come nigh, but the word of reconciliation be witnessed, and

---

7. Howgill, *Mysteries*, 35–36.

the word of faith which makes clean, and purifies, and sanctifies; where the old garment is put off, and the knowledge in the flesh denied, and the knowing in the life, in the spirit, where nothing comes to reign but life and power, where all is overturned, and with the power of the Lord comprehended, the dread and life of the living God, to whom be all honour and glory for ever.[8]

---

8. Fox, *Works*, 4:305.

Dynamics of Evil

And why is the devil, and they that be of him, called a deceiver, because he is out of the truth, and would draw others from and out of the truth, and so destroy them both body and soul, but Christ destroyeth him.—George Fox

IN STEVEN SPIELBERG'S 1994 film *Schindler's List,* there was a scene that has remained with me as an accurate portrayal of the dynamics of evil. This particular scene offered a glimpse into the suprahuman power of darkness that lies behind the temptation to evil to which we, as humans, are exposed and regularly succumb as a matter of course. The state or condition produced by such yielding to temptation is called in our tradition's parlance "worldliness," "the world" being the term that signifies humanity's opposition to God. George Fox writes: "All relations in the world are Devilish, Selfish, heathenish and earthly."[1]

The recalled scene from the film centers on an interaction between a commander of a camp and a young female Jewish engineer. She has discovered that one of the camp's buildings has a faulty foundation that will inevitably lead to the building's collapse, if not corrected. The scene begins with her rushing into the presence of the camp's commander and his men who listen to her confident, fervent warning. After the commander has heard her out, he pauses a moment to consider the situation, and then promptly orders one of his men to shoot her. The scene ends with her murder.

Nearly a quarter century after having first seen this film, I mistakenly recalled the woman being dragged away while continuing to protest the commander's failure to understand the danger: the building would collapse if nothing were done. Having recently again watched the film, I found a

---

1. *Epigraph.* Benson, *Notes,* D2 829. Benson, *Notes,* D1 826.

different, more powerful ending to the scene from what I had previously imagined.

The scene ends with the woman being shot, but immediately before her murder, she and the commander exchange one line each of dialogue. The brief exchange unmasks and displays the forces of good and evil that lay behind the conflict just played out between them. As the woman is forced to her knees prior to being shot, she defiantly asserts: "It will take more than that." To which the camp commander readily replies: "I'm sure you're right."

Her dying assertion ("It will take more than that.") implies the truth cannot be altered or destroyed by the silencing of those who speak it. Truth, the Word of God, is eternal and unchanging, and as such, it remains unaffected by that which was "a murderer from the beginning, and abode not in the truth."[2] In this scene, that point is made when the woman withstands the demonic assault by remaining grounded and speaking the truth until the end.

The commander's reply ("I'm sure you're right.") while mockingly affirming the right and the true, simultaneously conveys a readiness to continue destroying beings who—alone of all God's creatures—can know and speak truth. By ordering the murder of the truth-speaker, the commander unmasks a satanic defiance that would always have the exalted truth subjugated: whether that dominance is gained overtly by the killing of the body, as in this scene; or covertly, insidiously, through eliciting an overriding fear of diminishment or death.

Such fear quickly draws the mind away to creaturely self-service, and leaves the soul languishing unattended and desolate, its lifeline to God abandoned. For it is only in attentive relationship with God that the soul lives (John 17:3). The forfeiture of the living relationship with God is signified in our tradition by the term "the Fall of man." "[B]y their fall they came under another power, another image, another likeness, and another [g]od, even the [g]od of the world."[3]

Though there were many other scenes in the film where destruction occurred on a larger scale, this one scene stood out because of the stark depiction of the characteristics of evil, and not simply its consequences. As opposed to satanic evil, the distinguishing mark of human sin is weakness: a refusal to honor truth when tempted by the possibility of possessing

---

2. John 8:44 (King James Version; all subsequent citations are from this version).
3. Fox, *Works*, 8:136.

whatever one loves instead of truth. A weak succumbing to temptation is the mark of human sin. In this scene, however, we see not only human but also demonic evil, the origin of the temptation of human beings, who in weakness yield. Writes Emil Brunner in *Christian Doctrine of Creation and Redemption*:

> Human sin, thanks to the fact that we are not pure spirits, but body-mind creatures, is never "complete." Its negative "perfection" would be pure defiance, pure arrogance, that is purely spiritual sin. But our sin, thanks to the fact of our human constitution as "body-mind," is always a mixture of defiance and weakness, of tendency to temptation both on the side of the mind and of the senses.[4]

In its demonic form, evil is "perfect" defiance of God; it originates in the rebellion of "that being who could not endure not to be equal with God,"[5] and it manifests in willful rejection of the divine imperative to obey the God of truth. In fact, George Fox identifies the rejection of truth as the defining act by which the devil became the devil: "he became a devil by going out of truth and so became a murderer and a destroyer."[6]

Evil is perpetuated by tempting weak humans to reject the truth, and thus dishonor our Creator who has created us in his image, as beings enabled to discern and participate in truth, which is Christ (John 14:6). To abdicate our humanity's gift of the ability to know and participate in the truth, and thereby to defy God's will, is to become less than human; it is not to become more than human, as the Serpent enticed, "ye shall be as gods" (Gen 3:5). Fox expressed this loss of humanity in the following passage from his journal:

> Now some men have the nature of swine wallowing in the mire, and some men have the nature of dogs to bite both the sheep and one another; and some men have the nature of lions, to tear, devour, and destroy. And some men have the nature of wolves to tear and devour the lambs and sheep of Christ; and some men have the nature of the Serpent (that old adversary), to sting, envenom, and poison. "He that hath an ear to hear, let him hear," and learn these things within himself. And some men have the natures of other beasts and creatures, minding nothing but earthly and visible things, and feeding without the fear of God. Some men have

---

4. Brunner, *Doctrine Creation*, 139.
5. Brunner, *Doctrine Creation*, 145.
6. Nickalls, *Journal*, 212.

> the nature of an horse, to praunce and vapour in their strength, and to be swift in doing evil; and some men have the nature of tall, sturdy oaks, to flourish and spread in wisdom and strength, who are strong in evil, which must perish and come to the fire. Thus the evil is but one in all, but worketh many ways; and whatsoever a man's or woman's nature is addicted to that is outward, the Evil One will fit him with that, and will please his nature and appetite to keep his mind in his inventions, and in the creatures, from the Creator.[7]

Regardless of the extent of the consequences—whether vast societal destruction or a single lie confined to a single, corrupted mind—the dynamics of human evil are always the same: assent to temptation coupled with defiance. Its outward consequences are indicative only of its extent but not of its intrinsic character, for that is determined at its inception, not in its effects. That evil is first acceded to within underscores the inescapability of personal responsibility. Taking personal responsibility is the sole human act that can hinder both succumbing to personal sin as well as to the social sin of conformity, necessary for scapegoating and other grander-scaled, collective expressions of evil.

Holding the line, speaking the truth is the Christian's (Quaker's) obligation in the Lamb's War. If the God of Truth is honored in just one mind, heart, and soul, the world is not lost, as Jesus showed us by prototypal example. In this statement given before Pilate shortly before the end of his earthly life, Jesus identified his life's purpose not only for himself but for us all. "To this end was I born, and for this cause came I into the world, that I should bear witness unto the truth. Every one that is of the truth heareth my voice" (John 18:37).

Seventeenth-century Friends of the Truth heard his voice and preached the Word of reconciliation to the fallen world. And we continue, grounded and speaking the truth until the end.

> [T]he ministers of the word that preached that, preached the word that reconciled people to God, and did hammer down and cut down and burn up that which was in them and had made a separation betwixt them and God, so it's called the word of reconciliation and reconciles all things to God in one, both things in heaven and things in earth.[8]

---

7. Nickalls, *Journal*, 59.
8. Benson, *Notes*, WD 328.

The Rose That Bare Gesù

There is no rose of such virtue / As is the rose that bare Gesù.
For in this rose contained was / Heaven and earth in little space;
Res miranda [a wonderful thing].
The angels sungen the shepherds to / Gloria in excelsis Deo:
Gaudeamus. [Let us rejoice.]
Leave we all this worldly mirth / And follow we this joyful birth;
Transeamus. [Let us go across.]—Fifteenth-century English carol

THE ICONOGRAPHY OF THE Nativity story is rich with meaning, and the lyrics of this Renaissance carol touch upon some of that meaning in the opening verse: "There is no rose of such virtue / As is the rose that bare Gesù." Virtue is the quality that identifies the mother of Jesus; virtue carries and nurtures the seed, and to it gives birth. The incarnate God, Christ Within, is brought into being through spiritual gestation in virtue.

Our tradition doesn't rely on a single story to communicate the reality of our condition and the transformation that is our fulfillment, our new birth. The richness of its figuration offers many opportunities to imaginatively grasp and thereby learn what we're called to. "The Mediate Role of Virtue" is an essay on a different story in Scripture (found in Luke 16) that harbors the same theme of the necessity of virtue for the coming of the Lord.

The Mediate Role of Virtue

Love mercy and true judgment, justice and righteousness; for the Lord delighteth in such. Consider these things in time, and take heed how ye spend your time. Now ye have time, prize it; and show mercy, that ye may receive mercy from the Lord: for he is coming to try all things, and will plead with all flesh as by fire.—George Fox

THIS STATEMENT IS FROM a letter that Fox wrote in 1650 while he was being held in Darby jail. In this letter, Fox admonishes local judges to love virtue, specifically "mercy, true judgment, justice and righteousness." Notice that he does not reason with the judges about their duty, nor does he argue that virtuous behavior would benefit society. Both of these arguments would call upon the judges to choose virtue so that some ideal of character or society could be met. Fox, instead, gives different reasons for being virtuous: (1) the Lord delights in virtuous behavior; and conversely, (2) the Lord will judge and punish harshly those who refuse virtue: "[he] will plead with all flesh as by fire." Fox is claiming that virtue is a necessary mediate condition for receiving the proximate favor of God, not a practical measure for achieving some human ideal.

Implied in this understanding is the belief that there's some advantage to receiving God's favor and avoiding his wrath. Convincing people of this who are without the fear of God (that is to say, the knowledge of God) is difficult. It seems natural and obvious to the reprobate mind that each person must chart his own course toward maximum personal advantage, navigating around or conquering whatever obstacles impose themselves, even when those obstacles are the demands of virtue. Choosing virtue over opportunity for personal gain often does not seem wise to the man who

The Mediate Role of Virtue

does not know Christ: "for the children of this world are in their generation wiser than the children of light."[1]

That this worldly wisdom is, in fact, not life-enhancing but instead is life-inhibiting ignorance that can and must be contradicted is the primary theme of Scriptures and seventeenth-century Friends writings. Both sources hold up the pursuit and acquisition of virtue as an intermediate and necessary step that prepares one to receive eternal life, knowledge of the living God. This assertion is reinforced repeatedly throughout these writings, one example being the sixteenth chapter of Luke.

At the beginning of this chapter, Jesus tells a story of a man who is lacking in virtue: a steward who has been wasteful of his master's goods and, as a result, is fired. In straits for how he will live, the steward decides upon a plan: he will curry favor with those who owe his employer goods by reducing their liability. Not only does this steward lack prudence and economy, he also lacks the virtues of honesty and righteousness:

> How much owest thou unto my lord? And he said, An hundred measures of oil. And he said unto him, Take thy bill, and sit down quickly, and write fifty. Then said he to another, And how much owest thou? And he said, an hundred measures of wheat. And he said unto him, Take thy bill, and write fourscore (Luke 16:5b–7).

Once the man no longer has the job of steward, he will call upon these people for return favors: quid pro quo. The text then has the steward's employer evaluate the scheme: "And the lord commended the unjust steward, because he had done wisely" (16:8). How reasonable is it to praise fraud that has been injurious to oneself? The master praises the steward who cheated him; in a world devoid of virtue, reason also is in short supply.

This praise of the dishonest steward accelerates the chaos that began in the first line of the story: we were told that the steward was not doing what a steward does, which is care for his master's goods. When a word no longer signifies its meaning, confusion results. When a steward no longer cares for his master's goods, when a master praises his servant's thievery, chaos and confusion abound. In verse 9, this chaos crystallizes into a maxim: "And I say unto you, Make to yourselves friends of the mammon of unrighteousness; that, when ye fall, they may receive you into everlasting habitations."

At this point in the story when confusion is rife, having gained the apex and planted a senseless maxim as its flag, the narrative voice shifts.

---

1. *Epigrap*h. Fox, *Works*, 1:115. Luke 16:8b (King James Version; all subsequent citations are from this version).

Suddenly appearing in the passage's final verses (Luke 16:10–13) are cogent, inarguable assertions that follow one upon another. One senses that Jesus, having finished his story, is now presenting its moral:

> He that is faithful in that which is least is faithful also in much: and he that is unjust in the least is unjust also in much (16:10). If therefore ye have not been faithful in the unrighteous mammon, who will commit to your trust the true riches? (16:11) And if ye have not been faithful in that which is another man's, who shall give you that which is your own? (16:12) No servant can serve two masters: for either he will hate the one, and love the other; or else he will hold to the one, and despise the other. Ye cannot serve God and mammon (16:13).

With the exception of the first part of verse 10, all these statements are put into a negative rather than a positive form: "if ye have not been faithful" (16:11, 12); "[no] servant can serve"; "[y]e cannot serve" (16:13). One may state with assurance that a sinful (negative) condition will *not* enter the Kingdom, but one cannot positively state that behaving virtuously will ensure entry; for that entry is determined by God alone (Mark 13:32). We cannot assess whether we ourselves are virtuous; God alone, who is a consuming fire, tries the heart. Lack of virtue prohibits receiving Christ, but even one's very best effort to be virtuous does not guarantee the coming of Christ. For that, one can only prepare oneself, and then wait and watch (Mark 13:37).

Last First-day (Sunday) in worship at a meeting in Philadelphia, Pennsylvania, there were five messages given during the hour. Each contained a personal narrative which held up a particular virtue: benevolence, bravery, tolerance, empathy, and helpfulness. All the messages followed the same narrative arc: virtue was exhibited and virtue was rewarded. Embodying virtues is often rewarding, useful, and practical in shaping and improving our individual lives and of that of the social groups to which we belong. That is not, however, the reason for embodying virtue that either Jesus or first Friends give. For them, the condition of virtue is a mediate state, which is neither accommodated in the world nor yet given entry into heaven. Virtue's purpose and value is that it prepares the heart to be acceptable to God. Virtue affirms and signals a desire and humble willingness to sacrifice and then to wait upon the coming of the Lord. It is faith before faith is given.

In Him We Live, Move, and Have Our Being

IN THE PREFACE TO *Christianity and Civilisation,* first delivered as Gifford Lectures in 1946 and 1947, the Swiss theologian Emil Brunner tells of the purpose of this work: he sought "to formulate and to justify [his] conviction that only Christianity is capable of furnishing the basis of a civilisation which can rightly be described as human."[1] A civilization is largely determined by the prevailing answers that its various cultures give to basic questions about being; truth, time, man's place in the universe, meaning, justice, freedom, and creativity, and these are the topics Brunner examines in *Christianity and Civilisation*. In his lecture "The Problem of Meaning," he asserts:

> Apart from the answer of the Christian Gospel... the most important solution of the problem of meaning within Western history is that of Greek philosophy.[2]

Narrowing his exploration to these two worldviews, Brunner traces each of their origins and principles, and the effects of each upon Western civilization throughout historical periods and into our own modern time.

In this preface, Brunner speaks of his hesitancy to take on this work, feeling a disproportion between the topic and his "equipment for dealing with it," as it is a vast subject requiring expertise in many areas. He commits himself to this labor, however, as he believes it to be a topic in urgent need of explication.

A feeling of urgency likewise compels me to look at these two prevailing Western worldviews but within a greatly narrowed scope: one encounter between a minister of the Christian gospel and some Athenian philosophers: Paul's sermon given in the middle of the first century on the

---

1. Brunner, *Civilisation*, (v).
2. Brunner, *Civilisation*, 63.

Areopagus (Hill of Ares) to the Stoics and Epicureans, as recorded in Acts 17. This encounter is the earliest record of the Christian gospel confronting Greek humanism, and so Paul's impressions, actions, and statements are worth close examination, as they provide inspired insight into the fundamental differences between these two worldviews: differences that were apparent to each of their proponents but whose significance was fully understood only by the Apostle who, having been given Christ, the wisdom of God, had superseded the parameters of mind-bound philosophy. As George Fox said, "Many witness Christ in them in this age, as in the days of the apostles, which is above the heathen philosophers."[3]

Through this exercise, I hope to introduce Friends to the claim (or to substantiate it, for those already familiar) that original prophetic, primitive Christianity differs from the precepts informing Liberal Quaker belief and practice today, based as they are upon suppositions whose roots lie in Greek metaphysics, and not prophetic faith. The one thing needful—discovered, proclaimed, and suffered for by early Friends, as well as the prophets and apostles before them—has been lost to our religious society, and I hope that those who share my concern for reclaiming prophetic Quaker faith—or who are willing to hear more of this matter—will later turn to Brunner's writing for a more comprehensive treatment of the differences between these two worldviews.

In the following paragraphs, which are taken from his lecture "Man in the Universe," Brunner sets out the fundamental conception of Greek humanism; in the second paragraph, he presents the contrasting principle of Christian humanism:

> [Greek humanism] Man discovers in himself that which distinguishes him from the animal and nature as a whole and elevates him above, the Nous or the Logos, that spiritual principle which underlies all specifically human activity and gives man's work the character and content of human dignity. Now, this Nous or Logos is, at the same time, the principle which links mankind with the divine; the Logos is not merely the principle of human thought and meaningful action, but also that divine force which orders the world and makes it a Cosmos. It is the divine spark in human reason by which alone man emancipates himself from nature and places himself above it. It is that same divine spark in his reason in which he experiences the divinity of his innermost being. . . . Just as the divine Logos permeates nature and orders it, so it also

---

3. Fox, *Works*, 3:104.

permeates and orders man. But in man this divine principle becomes conscious knowledge. *It is in the recognition of himself as partaker in the divine Logos that man becomes conscious of his specific essence and value; his humanity is, at the same time, divinity.* [Italics in this and other quoted passages are mine.]

In biblical revelation the continuum of primitive mind is disrupted in an entirely different manner. . . . *God is no more the immanent principle of the world, but its Lord and Creator. He, the Lord-creator, alone is divine.* . . . Man in spite of every thing he has and is, with his spiritual as well as natural powers, is not divine. He is a creature. . . . Man alone is created in the image of God. . . . And this imago dei is the principle of Christian humanism as distinguished from Greek . . . *man's being created in the image of God does not imply any kind of divine spiritual substance in man, but only his relation to God.* . . . Christian humanism therefore, as distinguished from the Greek, is of such a kind that the humane character of existence is not automatically a possession of man, but is dependent on his relation to God, and remains a matter of decision.[4]

Some forms of false worship—idolatry—are easier to recognize than others: the lust and determination to secure social position and power; to indulge in animal sensuality; or to wield brute force are obvious signs of error. More difficult to discern are the indicators of a subtle idolatry in which natural human power is worshiped for its ability to orchestrate the good life, indicated by elevation of values and principles to highest prominence. Such idolatry is rarely challenged in Scripture, perhaps because it comes to the fore only when civic life is stable and free from grosser error. Paul's sermon on the Areopagus is the earliest example of a challenge to this form of idolatry, namely, a challenge to the proposition that divinity resides within human beings as a natural attribute.

Before beginning a verbatim account of Paul's sermon, the Scripture writer provides some background information about Paul's situation in Athens: While waiting for two helpers to join him, Paul assesses the spiritual condition of the city and finds its idolatry distressing. He goes to the synagogue to reason with both Jews and Gentiles, and argues in the marketplace with whoever is willing. He preaches the gospel of Jesus and the resurrection, and the philosophers are privately critical and insulting but

---

4. Brunner, *Civilisation*, 77–79.

curious to hear more. Then they all go to the Areopagus where Athenians regularly resort to hear the latest ideas, and Paul begins to preach:

> Ye men of Athens, I perceive that in all things ye are too superstitious. For as I passed by, and beheld your devotions, I found an altar with this inscription, TO THE UNKNOWN GOD. Whom therefore ye ignorantly worship, him declare I unto you.[5]

At the start of his sermon, Paul sets out a major difference between his faith and the condition of his hearers: Paul knows God, and the philosophers do not. The Athenians, by their own admission, claim God is "Unknown," and therefore, by implication, unknowable. It is experiential knowledge of God that enables us to worship him as he would be worshiped: in spirit and in truth. Jesus draws the connection between knowledge of God and true worship when he speaks to the Samaritan:

> Ye worship ye know not what: we know what we worship: for salvation is of the Jews. But the hour cometh, and now is, when the true worshippers shall worship the Father in spirit and in truth: for the Father seeketh such to worship him. God is a Spirit: and they that worship him must worship him in spirit and in truth (John 4:22–24).

Unlike the Greeks who worship an "Unknown God," Paul *does* know God, and is thus enabled to declare God's work and humanity's relation to him. The following precepts in Paul's sermon would have been foreign to the Athenians:

> God that made the world and all things therein, seeing that he is Lord of heaven and earth, dwelleth not in temples made with hands; Neither is worshipped with men's hands, as though he needed any thing, seeing he giveth to all life, and breath, and all things (Acts 17:24–25).

Paul contends that God is Creator and Lord, and thus the giver and ruler of life; man receives life and is subject to God's power. He is not, as the Greeks would have it, a builder and maker of ideas (notional speculations) or buildings (temples) that house God; for God does not dwell in temples made with hands (made by man). Rather, it is God who acts and reveals himself to man. We wait upon him to move, like the Spirit upon the face of the waters. We wait upon the Lord; this is the way of prophetic Quaker worship.

5. Acts 17:22b–23 (King James Version; all subsequent citations are from this version).

In Him We Live, Move, and Have Our Being

> And [God] hath made of one blood all nations of men for to dwell on all the face of the earth, and hath determined the times before appointed, and the bounds of their habitation; That they should seek the Lord, if haply they might feel after him, and find him, though he be not far from every one of us (17:26–27).

In saying that God has made "of one blood all the nations of men," Paul identifies man's condition as universal. What is the condition that is true for all people in all times and places? It is *the felt need for God*, not the possession of "that of God in every one," but *the need for God*. A sense of alienation from God suffuses each human psyche and leads to a search to overcome the corresponding anxiety that is felt by every person in every time and in every nation. God has decreed each person will feel his or her need for God, and, in feeling this need, should seek the Lord.

Idolatry corrupts the search. Some poor substitute for God is found, the soul assuaged, and the search stopped. Some item, some loyalty, some pleasure, some theory, some circumstance, some obligation, some obsession stands in for God, numbing or distracting man from his true feeling of need. God is ready to meet our need for him, and when he reveals himself, then, and only then, is our felt need truly met: life's meaning and fulfillment is known.

> For in him we live, and move, and have our being; as certain also of your own poets have said, For we are also his offspring (17:28).

We are his "offspring," a word denoting kinship, relationship. Says Brunner: "For man's being created in the image of God does not imply any kind of divine spiritual substance in man, but only *his relation to God*."[6] We are separate from but related to God: "He came unto his own, and his own received him not. But as many as received him, to them gave he power to become the sons of God" (John 1:11–12a).

> Forasmuch then as we are the offspring of God, we ought not to think that the Godhead is like unto gold, or silver, or stone, graven by art and man's device. And the times of this ignorance God winked at; but now commandeth all men every where to repent (17:29–30).

God has ever had a plan for humanity's restoration, Paul avers. Now the time is come that a new thing is commanded: repentance. We are to repent of our attributing divinity to ourselves ("ye shall be as gods" [Gen

---

6. Brunner, *Civilisation*, 78.

3:5]); that is, repent of the claim "that of God" resides within, when God is yet unknown, yet unrevealed. God is not mocked. True authority, the author of our faith, suffers outside the gate of our habitation, and we must become subject to his enlarging jurisdiction. The world in the human heart is judged:

> Because he hath appointed a day, in the which he will judge the world in righteousness by that man whom he hath ordained; whereof he hath given assurance unto all men, in that he hath raised him from the dead (Acts 17:31).

It is a foolish idea to the Greeks that a human being might be raised from the dead; it is beyond reason. For the Epicureans, death was the end of all things, and for the Stoics, death was followed by the soul being absorbed into that from which it sprang.

> But we preach Christ crucified, unto the Jews a stumblingblock, and unto the Greeks foolishness; But unto them which are called, both Jews and Greeks, Christ the power of God, and the wisdom of God (I Cor 1:23–24).

Paul speaks beyond the Greeks understanding, beyond their reason. Through repentance we condemn to death the reprobate mind: having seen that our inward condition is inadequate to meet our felt need. It is a universal verdict of the universal judgment appointed by God. We are given to know the risen one, even Christ Jesus, who is ordained by God to judge and to speak to this condition, this fallen state. We are raised to life in unity with him that has been raised from the dead. Beyond our comprehension, our reason, beyond our philosophy, we are given to know the inward resurrection experientially.

In the final words of his sermon, Paul presents the most conclusive difference between Christian faith and the philosophical mysticism of the Greeks. It is *a person* we encounter in the risen Christ, and this person, Christ Jesus, becomes the foundation for our life. Impersonal mystical openings occur, but only foreshadow the subsequent restoration of personal relationship with God, drawing us to Christ, his Word. Lewis Benson states in his essay "Prophetic Quakerism":

> Wherever the philosophical type of mysticism has found expression within the limits of the Christian community, it has sought to

> reduce the saving Word of God addressed inwardly by the Voice of Jesus Christ to something less personal.[7]

That seventeenth-century Friends understood the person of Jesus Christ to be inwardly revealed is apparent in George Fox's most frequently used phrase that expressed the basic tenet of Quaker faith: "Christ is come to teach his people himself." Christ is active: coming to us and teaching us as only a person can. The basic law of man's being is to live by the Word of God. We must come into an experiential knowledge of Jesus Christ, the Word of God.

The statements in Paul's sermon on the Areopagus accord with Jesus's and first Friends' teachings, because every one of them spoke from the same source: the knowledge and power of God. As their source was the gospel, the power of God, there was unity in their understanding.

- There is one God who is Creator and Lord (25-26).
- God has made all humanity to feel their need of him, for in relationship with him our being is completed and perfected (26-28).
- God is not like that which we can devise by thinking or making (29).
- It is time to repent and end the ignorance of idolatry (30).
- Each is to be judged in his spiritually deadened state and resurrected to life in Christ (31-32).

In the face of last century's Liberal Quaker communities turning away from prophetic faith and, in its stead, adopting a philosophy of values, Lewis Benson re-introduced the prophetic, primitive Christianity held forth by George Fox and other first Friends.

> The conversational relationship with God for which man was designated is essential to man's life. When this relationship is broken, the ground of man's life is broken and instead of life, he knows only death.... There is no coming out of darkness and death while man is alienated from God and does not listen to his word or fails to obey his command. This dialogic relationship to God is not a special religious consciousness but it is the basic law of man's being.[8]

---

7. Benson, *Truth is Christ*, 16.
8. Benson, *Catholic Quakerism*, 14.

Benson, Brunner, early Friends, and the apostle Paul all find unity in the truth of prophetic Christian faith. The unity of their understanding witnesses to the universality of God's call to each person to come into a conversational relationship with him and, furthermore, witnesses to the potential for each person to answer his call in righteousness. In every century, place, and culture, there are those of us who have come to know experientially the only true God, and Jesus Christ, whom he has sent, whom he raised from the dead, the one in whom we live, and move, and have our being.

On Presumption and Belief in John 11

OF THE TWENTY-ONE CHAPTERS in John's Gospel, chapter 11 has been for decades the least interesting to me. It was its scattered quality that put me off: too many characters, most of them contributing only snippets; vignettes that seemed to go nowhere; dialogue that just didn't connect or flow; inexplicable actions and reactions. Where was the throughline, I asked myself: the coherent theme that took shape with each succeeding verse.

As a narrative, this chapter seemed more like a script out of Theater of the Absurd, a movement that began in the late 1950s that took its cue from Existentialism, and featured works that showed the breakdown of communication and its replacement with irrational and illogical speech. It turns out, this impression was not so far from the truth: chapter 11 is about the breakdown of communication that occurs when people work exclusively from their own presumptions and complacent certainties. Unlike the works by the existentialists and the absurdists, however, this chapter not only illustrates the problem but shows the way out of it. Far from being a jumble of discord, this chapter has a tightly organized structure that showcases the dysfunction arising from human presumption.

INTRODUCTION OF THEME AND CHARACTERS

No time is wasted in setting up the forces at play in this narrative and the personae that represent those forces. The chapter begins:

> Now a certain man was sick, named Lazarus, of Bethany, the town of Mary and her sister Martha. (It was that Mary which anointed the Lord with ointment, and wiped his feet with her hair, whose brother Lazarus was sick.) Therefore his sisters sent unto him, saying, Lord, behold, he whom thou lovest is sick.[1]

---

1. John 11:1–3 (King James Version; all subsequent citations are from this version).

As readers of gospel narratives may have come to expect, Jesus sets out a succinct description of the situation and its end, its telos, which is not death but is instead, the glory of God: "This sickness is not unto death, but for the glory of God, that the Son of God might be glorified thereby" (John 11:4).

In these opening verses, we're told all is not well; there's sickness in the household: that is to say, there's sickness in the place where one dwells, and Jesus is sent for, because he is known to heal that which is not well in the place where one dwells: that is to say, Jesus heals the soul.

Mary and Martha are in close relationship with the sick one (just like the self is in close relationship with the soul!); as such, we will see later in the chapter how each of these different "selves" responds to the Lord. (We are given some foreshadowing when we're told early on that Mary attends to the Lord [anoints him and wipes his feet with her hair] but find no mention made of Martha.) These sisters—each in her own way—will represent a particular response to the Lord: one spiritual and the other spiritless. Interpreted, the chapter's first few verses tell us that a soul can be sick, and Jesus called upon; yet not every manner of being will reach to and engage him.

ILLUSTRATING THE PROBLEM

We will pick up this theme of the manner of being that does—or does not—reach to Jesus after first taking a detour to examine the sickness that Jesus is called upon to heal. We're given to see its nature: the natural human tendency to presume to know what is right and true when, in fact, one doesn't.

This segment starts with verse 5 and runs through 17. In these thirteen verses, there are several examples of what at first glance—and perhaps at second or third glance—appears to be confusion and absurdity. I'll briefly list these examples, as their significance lies not so much in each one separately but in their assembly into a unit, a few of the many varied expressions of the sickness that *is* unto death. Look for absurdity, confusion, and presumption in these verses.

Here we go:

1. Verses 5–6: "Now Jesus loved Martha, and her sister, and Lazarus. When he had heard therefore that he was sick, he abode two days still in the same place where he was."

On Presumption and Belief in John 11

Jesus's abiding two days in the same place after hearing Lazarus was sick seems to make no sense: he would want to get to Lazarus as quickly as possible is our presumption. Look how we are implicated in presumption right from the start! A little reasoning goes a long way—too far in fact, as we'll see confirmed later in the text.

2. Verses 7–10: "Then after that saith he to his disciples, Let us go into Judaea again. His disciples say unto him, Master, the Jews of late sought to stone thee; and goest thou thither again? Jesus answered, Are there not twelve hours in the day? If any man walk in the day, he stumbleth not, because he seeth the light of this world. But if a man walk in the night, he stumbleth, because there is no light in him."

The disciples presume Jesus should consider the danger of entering Judaea. Jesus's answer ("Are there not twelve hours in the day?") seems to absurdly miss the point.

3. Verses 11b–15: "Our friend Lazarus sleepeth; but I go, that I may awake him out of sleep. Then said his disciples, Lord, if he sleep, he shall do well. Howbeit Jesus spake of his death: but they thought that he had spoken of taking of rest in sleep. Then said Jesus unto them plainly, Lazarus is dead. And I am glad for your sakes that I was not there, to the intent ye may believe; nevertheless let us go unto him."

The disciples presume Lazarus sleeps, as Jesus has said so. Jesus seems to contradict himself, creating confusion.

4. Verse 16: "Then said Thomas, which is called Didymus, unto his fellow disciples. Let us also go, that we may die with him."

Thomas (Didymus), who represents being of two minds, would prefer to have the matter settled, and so presumes it is, assuring himself with a display of flamboyant resolve.

Verse 17 states a numerical fact ("Then when Jesus came, he found that he [Lazarus] had lain in the grave four days already."), and as math partakes of the absolute and certain, the numerical reference signals the end of this segment of confusion, which began in like manner with a similar numerical fact in verse 6 ("he abode two days still in the same place"); this befuddling segment is hemmed in on both sides with number facts, thereby containing the apparent disorder. We've been given a glimpse into the miscommunication, confusion, and absurdity that characterizes our natural condition, as well as our varied attempts to corral that disorder with fact and presumption. It is our "faith" in our own faculties to control the vicissitudes of life that is "the sickness unto death."

Nevertheless, Jesus's words throughout this section, though seeming to contribute to the confusion, are clear and consistent. I'll not go through all four examples one-by-one but will instead offer just one explanation: to the second example in the list (11:7–10):

Jesus has informed his disciples that they will go into Judaea to assist Lazarus, and they respond that there is danger there: possible stoning. Their presumption is that Jesus must assess the outward circumstances before deciding to act: are circumstances favorable? dangerous? worth the risk? Although Jesus's answer seems to have nothing to do with their question ("Are there not twelve hours in the day? If any man walk in the day, he stumbleth not, because he seeth the light of this world. But if a man walk in the night, he stumbleth, because there is no light in him" [9–10]), his response does answer their concern. For he is teaching that one's actions should not derive from one's assessment of outward circumstance, as the disciples presume, but instead from inward direction found through "the light of this world."

THE SELF THAT PRESUMES AND THE SELF THAT WAITS

Now we can return to the theme of the manner of being that does—or does not—reach to Jesus. The next passage in the chapter (11:18–35) features a contrast between the opposing ways the self can function: the first, characterized by Martha, is the proud, arrogant self whose presumption fills up the self, puts itself forward, and spills out its presumptions onto others; and the second, characterized by Mary, is the humbled, empty self that waits to be given, to be filled with what she knows she does not herself possess. The distinction between the two is made immediately: "Then Martha, as soon as she heard that Jesus was coming, went and met him: but Mary sat still in the house" (11:20).

Conversely, Mary comes out to meet Jesus only after first learning that she has been called: "And when she [Martha] had so said, she went her way, and called Mary her sister secretly, saying, The Master is come, and calleth

On Presumption and Belief in John 11

for thee. As soon as she heard that, she arose quickly, and came unto him" (11:28–29).

Martha "went her [own] way," and there's evidence of her self-direction in her encounter with Jesus, who can teach her nothing. Look how frequently she presumes, using the words "I know":

> Then said Martha unto Jesus, Lord, if thou hadst been here, my brother had not died. But *I know*, that even now, whatsoever thou wilt ask of God, God will give it thee. Jesus saith unto her, Thy brother shall rise again. Martha saith unto him, *I know* that he shall rise again in the resurrection at the last day (11:21–24).

Jesus's response ("I am the resurrection, and the life") completely glances off her, and she falls back onto her stockpiled "knowledge," which bears no relevance to the powerful words she's just heard. With all the assurance of ignorance, she repeats her catechism: "Yea, Lord: I believe that thou art the Christ, the Son of God, which should come into the world" (11:27).

Although Mary's encounter with Jesus begins with the same words her sister spoke ("Lord, if thou hadst been here, my brother had not died" [11:32, 21]), she utters these words having first fallen down at his feet (11:32). Her spirit is humble, as we learned early in the chapter when she was first introduced: lowly, wiping his feet with her hair (11:2). Unlike her sister, she doesn't presume to be higher than she is, neither in knowledge nor in life. So low and empty of life is she that she weeps her emptiness before the Lord. And he, sensing the depth of her sorrow at loss of life, is reached, joins with her, and likewise weeps (11:35). It is the felt despair that—if we're honest—comes to us in our earthly life, and does elicit the Lord's compassionate response, his unity with us, and we feel his love.

THE PREVALENCE OF PRESUMPTION

To emphasize the prevalence of the error of presumption, we are given yet more examples. The "Jews" fare no better in this chapter than they do in the rest of John's Gospel. Here they as a group have a single voice and form a kind of backdrop chorus that stands for humankind in general, repeatedly in error to the point of comic absurdity. Situated midway between the accounts of each sister's meeting with Jesus are the Jews . . . presuming they know: "The Jews... when they saw Mary... went out, followed her, saying, She goeth unto the grave to weep there" (11:31).

Mary is not going to the grave but is going to find Jesus, who has called for her. Later presuming again, the Jews mistake the cause of Jesus's tears: that he weeps out of love for Lazarus (11:36), rather than his sorrow and rage at the misbegotten suffering he's sees in front of him. More presumption follows, as the Jews speak among themselves about Jesus's supposed failure to prevent Lazarus's death: "Could not this man, which opened the eyes of the blind, have caused that even this man should not have died?" (11:37).

And Martha, who from the start has modelled the presumptuous mode of being, again speaks after the Lord has commanded the stone that seals the cave where Lazarus lay be taken away. She does not surprise us when she jumps in with yet another mistaken presumption, this time relying on absolute, certain mathematical fact: "Lord, by this time he stinketh: for he hath been dead four days" (11:39b). Jesus's gentle reminder to her goes unanswered—and likely unheeded. "Said I not unto thee, that, if thou wouldest believe, thou shouldest see the glory of God?" (11:40).

BELIEF VERSUS PRESUMPTION

At key points in this chapter, Jesus has spoken of belief: he gives his reason for not immediately setting out to assist Lazarus, his intent being that his disciples might *believe* (11:15); he identifies *belief* as necessary for coming out of spiritual death and into life, and remaining there: "I am the resurrection, and the life: he that believeth in me, though he were dead, yet shall he live: And whosoever liveth and believeth in me shall never die" (11:25–26).

Belief is needed to see "the glory of God" (11:40); he states the cause for voicing his gratitude to the Father for having heard him: that his hearers might *believe* that he had been sent (11:42). Finally, the story ends with our being told "many of the Jews which came to Mary" (interpreted, which came to Mary's condition), and had seen the things which Jesus did, believed on him" (11:45).

It is in verses 41 and 42 that we see the crucial distinction made between belief and presumption, which is the overriding lesson of this narrative. Jesus says:

> Father, I thank thee that thou hast heard me. And I knew that thou hearest me always: but because of the people which stand by I said it, that they may believe that thou hast sent me.

Verb tenses are important here as they indicate timing: past, present, or future. (This is one example of the King James Version providing the necessary nuance to enable sound interpretation.) Jesus knows he has been heard by the Father—not that he *will be heard*, or that he *is heard* but that he *has been heard* (past tense). Whereas presumption gets out ahead of what is known; belief follows behind what *has been known*; belief is a result of experience, presumption the result of intellectual speculation.

The second sentence is also in the past tense: Jesus does not say, I know that thou hearest me always, but "I *knew* (past) that thou hearest me always." He does not speak so that the Father *will hear* him, for then his speaking would be a presumption on his part; rather he "*knew*" (past) that he is heard "always." He said ("Father, I thank thee that thou hast heard me" [11:41]) so that others may hear/believe that the Father has sent him (11:42). And surely they will have done so (future perfect!), when they too *have seen* (past) the power of God raise one from the dead, and *having seen* (past) Jesus's part in the action, they may now believe—not presume—that he has been sent by the Father.

One becomes able to distinguish intellectual presumption from experiential belief when one has been called forth by Christ into life, as was Lazarus (11:43). Then setting aside the trappings of the grave and spiritual death, that is to say, setting aside presumptuous, self-affirming tendencies, we have learned to wait in emptiness of soul, in the spiritual tomb where we dwell, anticipating the freedom afforded to each of us when we have felt the decree: "Loose him, and let him go." In that resurrection to life, we see the glory of God, and we glorify his Son whom we have known. "This sickness is not unto death, but for the glory of God, that the Son of God might be glorified thereby" (11:4).

On Redemption in John 11

He who expects to arrive at . . . the union of the soul with God, by means of consolation and comfort, will find himself mistaken. For, having sinned, we must expect to suffer, and be in some measure purified, before we can be in any degree fitted for a union with God, or permitted to taste the joy of his presence. Be ye patient, therefore, under all the sufferings which your Father is pleased to send you. If your love to him be pure, you will not seek him less in suffering than in consolation.—*A Guide to True Peace*

THIS ESSAY IS ABOUT the final stage in the process of redemption: when we have observed and embodied the demands of the Law; when we have heeded faithfully the requirements of conscience; when we have watched and waited expectantly, and yet have come up empty, and not known why. I will examine crucial verses in John 11 that point to the condition that immediately precedes the inward resurrection to life eternal. This chapter in John is about Lazarus being raised from the dead, but the verses I will focus on replicate the conditions of inward death and inward resurrection that are to be visited upon all.

THE MEANING OF *EMBRIMÁOMAI*

"When Jesus therefore saw her weeping, and the Jews also weeping which came with her, he groaned in the spirit, and was troubled."[1] Because the King James Version doesn't translate verse 33 well ("he groaned in the spirit, and was troubled" [33b]), I'll be using instead a literal translation of

---

1. *Epigraph*. Molinos et al. *Guide*, 54. John 11:33 (King James Version).

the New Testament by Richmond Lattimore, whose translation I'll identify by his initials: "RL." In his preface, Lattimore describes his technique:

> I have held throughout to the principle of keeping as close to the Greek as possible, not only for sense and for individual words, but in the belief that fidelity to the original word order and syntax may yield an English prose that to some extent reflects the style of the original.... [M]y aim has been to let all of my texts translate themselves with as little interference as possible.[2]

Lattimore's translation of verses 32 and 33 reads: (I've put the relevant sentence in italics.)

> When Mary came to where Jesus was, and saw him, she fell at his feet, saying to him: Lord, if you had been here, my brother would not have died. When Jesus saw her weeping, and saw the Jews who had come with her weeping, *he raged at his own spirit, and harrowed himself.*

The Greek word in question is "*embrimáomai.*" Whereas the King James Version translates this word as a gentle groan ("he groaned in the spirit"), Lattimore translates it as an intense, explosive anger: "he raged at his own spirit." Lattimore's choice is supported by New Testament scholar Rudolf Schnackenburg, who wrote: "The word [*embrimáomai*] indicates an outburst of anger, and any attempt to interpret it in terms of an internal emotional upset caused by grief, pain, or sympathy is illegitimate."[3]

The text itself supports these scholars' findings: The Jews interpret Jesus's weeping as arising from grief ("Then the Jews said: See how he loved him" [11:36 RL].), but as the Jews in this story always come to the wrong conclusion, we can assume that here their reasoning about Jesus's weeping is also wrong. Finally, *Word Study Greek-English New Testament* informs us that "*embrimáomai*" means "indignation."[4]

UNIVERSALITY OF BLAMING

Indignation and fault-finding is what Mary does: finding Jesus along the road, she greets him with an accusation: "Lord, if you had been here, my brother would not have died" (11:32 [RL]). Blame follows loss and suffering,

---

2. *New Testament.* Translated by Lattimore (vii, ix).
3. Schnackenburg, as quoted in Duvall.
4. *Greek-English New Testament*, s.v. embrimáomai.

a pattern of behavior not unique to Mary. Her sister Martha speaks the same words when she confronts Jesus. The repetition implies both react to loss and suffering in the same way: with resentment and blame (11:21 [RL]). That resorting to blame be seen as a universal and not solely a family characteristic, we're told that the Jews also suffer (11:33 [RL]) and blame Jesus: "Could not he, who opened the eyes of the blind man, make it so that this man also might not die?" (11:37 [RL]) We cannot miss the idea that loss, suffering, and resentment universally fuel blame. (It's the property of the first Adam—the one who blamed Eve—the one who blamed the Serpent.) Given all the examples in this eleventh chapter, we find the question of whether or not one dies to the self depends upon whether, having suffered loss, one chooses or refuses to cast blame elsewhere.

ANOTHER WAY

Verse 33 presents Jesus modeling a new and different way to handle loss: "he [Jesus] raged at his own spirit, and harrowed himself." Like the rest of humankind ("natural children of wrath" [Eph 2:3 (RL)]), Jesus rages at life's limits, rage that is typically redirected outward. ("If you had been here, my brother would not have died," say each of Lazarus's sisters.) Always quick to blame another for one's suffering, one assumes if only others changed—or were manipulated, controlled, or somehow gotten rid of—one would not have to suffer.

Jesus upends this fallacy by instead choosing to embody the human frailty and limitation without casting responsibility for it elsewhere: he feels the weakness that comes with loss; acknowledges the finitude that leads to suffering; and endures the rage of resentment that follows. Instead of looking outward to blame another, however, he holds the awareness of his finitude and endures; that is the meaning of "he . . . harrowed himself": he subjected himself to the distress and torment incumbent upon his being mortal and refused to obscure or deny it by looking for externalities to hold accountable. In short, he refused to blame. This is what it means to take on the sins of the world—whether grand or small—and absorb their effect, which will be loss to the self, its fleshly image and temporal equilibrium in the world. Absorbing the effects of sin is nicely described in these verses from First Peter:

> [H]e did no wrong, nor was any treachery found in his utterance;
> he was reviled and did not revile in answer; he suffered and spoke

no threats but gave himself up to him who judges justly (2:22–23 [RL]).

Returning to the passage in John, we are told: "Jesus once more was inwardly raging and went to the tomb" (11:38 [RL]). The rage accompanies one all the way to the tomb, wherein lies death to the self. God raises a person up from there . . . and from there only. The risen Christ abiding within restores abundant well-being (life eternal), and thereby, is the sin of the world borne and overcome.

THE INWARD RESURRECTION: JOHN 11:42

> So they took away the stone. And Jesus lifted up his eyes and said: Father, I thank you for hearing me, and I know that you always hear me; but because of the crowd which surrounds me, I said it so that they should believe that you sent me (11:41–42 [RL]).

Jesus knows the Father hears him, even when he doesn't speak aloud. Their communication is in the inward parts; he speaks aloud only that the crowd might hear. His spirit spoken (the apex of words!) manifests the unity of God and man, and enables others to sense and believe in God's power to send his Word to us. Such is prophetic ministry, as understood by Friends. It is the manifestation of the inward resurrection to life in Christ; that is to say, it is faith heard: "faith cometh by hearing, and hearing the word of God" (Rom 10:17 [KJV]).

[S]HALL HE FIND FAITH ON THE EARTH? (LUKE 18:8B [KJV])

Some have the form of godliness, acknowledging the need to undergo the cross within, yet in their hearts reject it, seeing no more than a stumbling block or foolishness (1 Cor 1:23). This is hypocrisy: dwelling in form without substance. Others go on with their worldly lives, having no sense of what they've forfeited, and one feels their loss, their emptiness, with compassion. Some from an early age have so felt truth's pervasive demand that the cross has been with them, a constant companion, though for a time unnamed. And there are some worthy folks who begin to feel truth's insistence after long years spent captivated by other concerns: social position; empty, intellectual notions; worship of power, or other idols. These folks mend, as they find the peace that comes with living authentically. Other conditions and paths could be listed, but whatever the variation, there is one universal constant that is observed in every soul that enters its rightful place in unity with God: suffering in and for the truth.

Some Observations on John's Second Epistle

For many deceivers have come forth into the world, who do not acknowledge the coming of Jesus Christ in the flesh; such is the deceiver and the antichrist. Look to yourselves, so as not to lose what we have done but receive your full reward. Whoever breaks forward and does not abide by the teaching of the Christ does not have God; the one who abides by his teaching has the Father and the Son. If anyone comes to you and does not bring this doctrine, do not take him into your house, and do not give him any greeting; for anyone who gives him a greeting shares in his evil deeds (2 John 1:7–11).

RECENTLY A FRIEND AND I were discussing the second epistle of John. She had brought up the above passage and was specifically interested in the seventh verse: "For many deceivers have come forth into the world, who do not acknowledge the coming of Jesus Christ in the flesh; such is the deceiver and the antichrist" (1:7 [RL]). And within that verse, the phrase "the coming of Jesus Christ in the flesh" stood out for her. "Do you have an idea of what this means?" she asked.

Just a few days before, I'd read this epistle and had thought about the very verse she'd pointed out. I suggested that the words "in the flesh" did not refer to Jesus's earthly life of a few decades. Rather, it seemed to me, the apostle was alluding to the presence of Christ Within; it was *our flesh*—the believers' flesh—to which the Light of Christ is come. And acknowledgment that Christ is come in the flesh is predicated upon that inward encounter with him, with his Presence.

A week or so later, my thought was confirmed when I read one of Fox's tracts titled "A Word," from which the following sentence is taken:

The Light That Is Given

"Who loves the light that he hath given them, witness Jesus Christ come in the flesh . . . and you that hold up the figures, deny Christ come in the flesh."[1] Loving the light Jesus Christ has given us (having first received it!) is inherent in any authentic witness that Jesus Christ is come in the flesh. And conversely, to "hold up the figures" ("figures" being antecedent forms bearing likeness to Christ) is to "deny Christ come in the flesh."

Those not having known this encounter/revelation can only posture an attitude of faith, and thus deserve the designation the apostle gives them: "deceivers." John sought to distinguish between those who'd experienced the arrival of Christ Within and those "deceivers" or "antichrists" (signifying enemies of Christ) who had not. In short, John was telling us that the essential defect of "the deceiver and the antichrist" is profession without possession.

> Whoever breaks forward and does not abide by the teaching of the Christ does not have God; the one who abides by his teaching has the Father and the Son (1:9 [RL]).

To "abide by the teaching of the Christ" is to learn from the one who "is come to teach his people himself," Christ who inwardly reveals himself that we may learn the Father's will and do it. And "whoever breaks forward," and distances him- or herself from this condition of hearing obedience, "does not have God" but are instead "presumptuous talkers of God, who see him not."[2] "Do not take him [the deceiver] into your house" (1:10 [RL]) is a warning to readers to keep some distance between themselves and deceivers, but the warning can also be interpreted figuratively. One must not allow a conceptual approach to faith to enter and occupy the living space where only an experience of faith should reside.

The apostle knows the danger of losing "what we have done" (1:8 [RL]) and cautions rigorous care when dealing with conceptual faith and those who harbor it: to refuse to offer even a greeting. For to greet is to acknowledge, and thus, in a minor way, to sanction. And to sanction deceit even in a minor way is to participate in and promote it: "for anyone who gives him a greeting shares in his evil deeds" (1:11 [RL]).

> That mind, which doth speak of God, but lives not, dwells not, nor abides in the fear of God, that mind must suffer, and pass under the

---

1. *Epigraph.* 2 John 1:7–11 (The New Testament translated by Richmond Lattimore [RL]). Fox, *Works*, 433.

2. Fox, *Works*, 4:30.

judgment of God, for the curse of God is upon that mind.... And that mind may talk of God, and speak of God, but not in union with God, nor from enjoyment of God in the spirit, nor from having purchased the knowledge of him through death and sufferings; but from hear-say of him, and from custom and tradition.³

Thus far this essay has considered the second half of John's epistle, which, with its warning about deceivers and antichrists stands in contrast to the epistle's first half, concerned as it is with truth and love. See how frequently the word "truth" appears in the epistle's first sentence: (Italics are mine.)

> The elder unto the elect lady and her children, whom I love in the *truth*; and not I only, but also all they that have known the *truth*; For the *truth's* sake, which dwelleth in us, and shall be with us for ever.⁴

Love is the outgoing expression of truth, which resides within, and thus not only does the apostle express his own love for the "elect lady" but is confident that "all they that have known the truth" will also love her: not because she elicits his or their affection but because the truth dwells within them and is the living source and impetus of love.

> And now I beseech thee, lady, not as though I wrote a new commandment unto thee, but that which we had from the beginning, that we love one another. And this is love, that we walk after his commandments. This is the commandment, That, as ye have heard from the beginning, ye should walk in it (1:5–6 [KJV]).

In verse 5, we read that love for one another is commanded, and has been so "from the beginning": the beginning referring to that glorious, singular event when one is "born . . . of God" (John 1:13 [KJV]). And so to love is to bring forth, to express, the Life that began and is continuing in Christ, the Truth.

In verse 6, a significant distinction is made between (1) the inward hearing of the Source and (2) its conveyance outward into the world. This distinction is made by the use of one letter: the letter "s" added to the word "commandment," making the word either singular or plural. The Source is one, and to attend to that Source is the one commandment (no "s" added). The expression of that Source will vary according to whatever teaching

---

3. Fox, *Works*, 7:32.
4. 1 John 1:1–2 (King James Version).

or guidance he gives at particular times and places: that is, there will be various, specific commandments (and so an "s" is added). These commandments (with an "s") are what we Quakers call "continuing revelation." So verses 5 and 6 diagram the economy of parousaic revelation: the Source being God, the Father, and the various, particular expressions of his person being love brought into the world through his Son, his substance and body: the elect people of God.

> Beloved, let us love one another: for love is of God; and every one that loveth is born of God, and knoweth God (1 John 4:7 [KJV]).

Some Observations on Revelation 10:5–7

And the angel which I saw stand upon the sea and upon the earth lifted up his hand to heaven, And sware by him that liveth for ever and ever, who created heaven, and the things that therein are, and the earth, and the things that therein are, and the sea, and the things which are therein, that there should be time no longer: But in the days of the voice of the seventh angel, when he shall begin to sound, the mystery of God should be finished, as he hath declared to his servants the prophets (Rev 10:5–7).

These verses from Revelation have a majesty about them. Something of gravity and magnificence is being revealed by this "mighty angel come down from heaven" (10:1). As such, his words are given the appropriate frame of reference: the earliest story we have in Scripture, the Creation story in Genesis. This passage from Revelation draws upon images and words that are recounted in the story of Creation. Thus we're being told that the angel's message is of highest importance—on par with Creation itself.

Not only do these verses from Revelation refer to the Creator and his first work, but they also develop particular elements found in the Creation story. For example, in verse 5, the evangelist tells us that he sees the angel stand with one foot upon the sea and one foot on the earth. The statement alludes to the verse in Genesis where the land is divided from the sea:

> And God said, Let the waters under the heaven be gathered together unto one place, and let the dry land appear: and it was so. And God called the dry land Earth; and the gathering together of the waters called he Seas: and God saw that it was good (Gen 1:9–10).

The angel bridges previously separated areas. Where there was division of land from sea, there is now connection through the angel's stance: "his right foot upon the sea, and his left foot on the earth" (Rev 10:2). The act is of such portent that the words bear repeating, which the evangelist does in verse 5.

In Creation, God differentiates one thing from another, such as land from water. (See other divisions in Genesis 1 in verses 4, 6, 7, 14, and 18.) Division separates: whereas "one" implies unity and resolution, "two" suggests movement, change, comparison, or activity: for example, up/down, lesser/greater, solid/fluid, left/right, etc. With the appearance of the angel, the division of two earth surfaces—land and sea—is bridged: that is to say, figuratively they are made one. With his stance, the angel transcends the structure of Creation and presages unity and wholeness. When fulfillment is come, when "the mystery of God [is] finished" (Rev 10:7), there is unity; there is peace and rest.

Another item presented in the first chapter of Genesis and addressed in these few verses from Revelation is the element of time: (The angel swears "by him that liveth for ever and ever . . . that there should be time no longer" [6].) In Genesis, time is introduced through the numbering of days that follow each specific creative act. (See verses 5, 8, 13, 19, 23, and 31.) For example, "And the evening and the morning were the first day" (Gen 1:5). Things are created in sequence, and time marks each change, activity, and division, like a poem's refrain, anchoring and imbuing each stanza.

Verse 6 in the Revelation passage shows the power and authority the eternal God has over time: "that there should be time no longer." The angel states God's intent to eliminate that element of Creation which separates him from his mortal creature. No longer is humanity to be a time-bound captive to death and separated from life eternal. Fox wrote:

> Ye coming out of that which was in time, ye come up to God, who was before time was. This is a mystery, he that can receive it let him.[1]

Through his stance and words, the mighty angel tells us the coordinates of space and time, which have previously defined our life, set our bounds as creatures, no longer hold sway. Where we have been formerly is not where we are now to be: outside of time and in unity with God.

---

1. *Epigraph.* Rev 10:5–7 (King James Version; all subsequent citations are from this version). Fox, *Works,* 7:57.

Some Observations on Revelation 10:5–7

A PRECIOUS STATE

In the following quotation, Fox identifies time as the element in which all "troubles, persecutions, and temptations" occur, and he presents the alternative: the safety of the everlasting power of the Lord. As one would expect, Fox's understanding is in agreement with the angel's message of moving beyond time into that power that is everlasting and over all. "All trials, troubles, persecutions and temptations, came up in time; but the Lord's power, which is everlasting, is over all such things, in which is safety."[2]

Upon awakening very early in the morning this past "time called Christmas," I was surprised to receive a gift. It was an insight: All I had experienced in my life was to a single end, and that end was to know and be in unity with God. Taking this newly given, trustworthy certainty into my barely conscious mind led to a delightful first thought of the day: that all the calamities, tragedies, and effort, all the betrayals, injuries, and mistakes I had made and endured from others . . . all of it had been ultimately to good purpose. All the mini-narratives I had composed and accumulated—drawn from my earliest memory to those of yesterday—did not define my being but were instead a kind of school to bring me to everlasting life, where true being is known. Furthermore, whatever remaining trials were to come, I could accept with quiet assurance, lightly and gracefully, for all was in good order, and the end was, and would ever be, life in Christ.

> He who feels the covenant in Christ and life streaming into his heart through the covenant, and the seal of eternal peace to his soul, and that he shall never be left nor forsaken by the fountain of mercy, but all that ever befalls him shall conduce towards the working out of the perfect redemption and salvation of his soul; this is a precious state indeed; and this is the state which the feeling of the faith, and the living obedience in the Spirit leads to.[3]

---

2. Benson, *Notes*, H8 766.
3. Penington, *Works*, 2:268.

Increase our Faith
Some Observations on Luke 17:1–10

Then said he unto the disciples, It is impossible but that offences will come: but woe unto him, through whom they come! It were better for him that a millstone were hanged about his neck, and he cast into the sea, than that he should offend one of these little ones. Take heed to yourselves: If thy brother trespass against thee, rebuke him; and if he repent, forgive him. And if he trespass against thee seven times in a day, and seven times in a day turn again to thee, saying, I repent; thou shalt forgive him. And the apostles said unto the Lord, Increase our faith (Luke 17:1–5).

ONE OF THE MORE difficult facts of life is that "offences will come." Being on the receiving end of an offense and mulling over the injustice suffered from another's selfish or wicked act, one is likely to find that one's equanimity and focus have been lost. This loss of orientation is recognized and conveyed in Richmond Lattimore's more literal translation of the first verse of this passage: "It is impossible that there should come no causes to make man go astray."[1]

This literal rendering foregrounds the danger to the soul that results from having undergone an offense: the wounded soul may "go astray." Having suffered injury, the soul is tempted to covet and use power to restore its broken equanimity in what seems like just retribution. Brandishing power over others in order to restore a sense of self perpetuates the offense. And this dynamic repeated indefinitely becomes a de facto principle

---

1. *Epigraph*. Luke 17:1–5 (King James Version [KJV]). Luke 17:1 (The New Testament translated by Richmond Lattimore [RL]).

undergirding human interaction, and results in a world of fear, anger, and misuse of power. "[T]he whole world lieth in wickedness" (1 John 5:19 [KJV]), thereby ensuring that, as Jesus said, "offenses will come."

In this passage, Jesus walks his disciples through this problem and into the solution. He begins by addressing the issue of justice: the offender has trespassed a boundary; violated an understood agreement, spoken or not; and caused misery to another who is innocent. Though accountable, he himself seems not to have suffered at all. Not so, says Jesus; there is justice within, and the offender can expect great misery:

> [W]oe unto him, through whom [offenses] come! It were better for him that a millstone were hanged about his neck, and he cast into the sea, than that he should offend one of these little ones (Luke 17:1b–2 [KJV]).

Being sunk into the darkness and chaos of the sea (with a millstone necklace!) with no firm ground nor hope of life is the justice meted out to the offender's soul. The victim's sense that the miscreant should suffer for his misdeed as much or more than he himself has suffered is satisfied by Jesus's pronouncement; in the soul, justice is served. Not only does this vivid image of punishment reassure the victim that an equal or greater suffering will come to the wrongdoer, but it also warns him to stand guard against the temptation to likewise become an offender and undergo such a punishment himself. Jesus would put a stop to the chain reaction of victim becoming offender.

Assuring the disciples that inward justice will always be in force, Jesus stills the impulse to take retribution, to pay back. As an alternative to this natural destructive impulse, he then sets out a rightly ordered procedure for handling offenses:

> Take heed to yourselves: If thy brother trespass against thee, rebuke him; and if he repent, forgive him. And if he trespass against thee seven times in a day, and seven times in a day turn again to thee, saying, I repent; thou shalt forgive him (17:3–4 [KJV]).

The soul speaking truth to power disencumbers itself of the burden of injustice and puts it in the open. Should the offense have been unintended, the misunderstanding is brought to light and can be explained. If the wrongdoer recognizes that he's overstepped the boundary, behaved unjustly, and in the future is willing to abide by agreed limits—signaled by his repentance—then forgiving is in order. Conversely, if there's a refusal to recognize acceptable limits and no repentance forthcoming, the relationship is not to be restored.

These are all principles that can be practiced using the powers available to our nature: reason and conscience can get us this far. Beyond the restoration of relationship by truth-telling and re-affirming social boundaries, however, is a call to handle offenses in a way that requires more than human ability. Jesus calls us and the disciples to this new way: to reframe the event and see it differently; to see it through the perspective of faith, rather than perspective of our limited worldly nature. Doing so will enable us to see that we can lose nothing that can truly affect our well-being.

When the events of life are seen through the eye of faith, one cannot be deprived of anything necessary for one's happiness. If one's treasure is in heaven, can anyone break in and steal? No. It is only when there is a failure to see that one's treasure is in heaven that one can be rattled or devitalized by worldly loss. Living in faith, no power or principalities

> nor things present, nor things to come. Nor height, nor depth, nor any other creature shall be able to separate us from the love of God, which is in Christ Jesus our Lord (Rom 8:38–39 [KJV]).

Living in a world where offenses inevitably come, the disciples feel their well-being to be under threat. They also intuit that faith is the sole guarantee of their inward peace . . . if they just had enough of it. So sensibly, they ask of Jesus: "Increase our faith" (Luke 17:5 [KJV]). Jesus responds:

> If ye had faith as a grain of mustard seed, ye might say unto this sycamine tree, Be thou plucked up by the root, and be thou planted in the sea; and it should obey you (17:6 [KJV]).

Implied in the disciples' request for increased faith is the assumption they already have a certain degree of faith, and they just need more. Jesus corrects them: If they had even a tiny amount of faith (even as "a grain of mustard seed"), they could do a mighty act of power: they could command a tree to uproot itself and be "planted in the sea; and it should obey." (Note the echoing imagery: the offender who sinks in the sea [2] and the tree, which, through faith, can thrive there [6].) Man's lack of faith entails a lack of power over nature: his own human nature. Without faith, man has no power to avoid disorder and weakness, and he sinks into the chaos of external threats, the offences that are bound to come, and into the ocean of darkness.

Having faith, he can thrive even when planted in the chaos of the world that lies in wickedness, even as a sycamine tree could be planted in a hostile environment of the sea. Having faith, the hearing/obeying relationship with his Creator, man is restored, strengthened, and empowered to withstand and rise above such assaults upon his soul. He is given the power of God to rule over his human nature and to thrive regardless of the circumstances.

Though the disciples think they already have faith and simply need more, Jesus knows faith to be something other than what the disciples understand by the word. Likewise, the seventeenth-century Friends carefully distinguished the difference between what was commonly thought to be faith and the meaning given to the word by Jesus. Penington asserts: (Emphasis is his.)

> That *the true faith* (the faith of the gospel, the faith of the elect, the faith which saves the sinner from sin, and makes him more than a conqueror over sin and the powers of darkness) *is a belief in the nature of God*; which belief giveth entrance into, fixeth in and causeth an abiding in that nature.... And nothing can believe in the nature, but what is one with the nature. So then faith is not a believing the history of the scripture ... or a believing that Christ died for sinners in general, or for me in particular ... but a uniting to the nature of God in Christ.[2]

Faith is "a belief in the nature of God"... which causes "an abiding in that nature." It is "a uniting to the nature of God in Christ" that is the true faith which keeps us in peace, empowered to withstand all the assaults that will come. In the final verses of this passage, Jesus instructs the disciples in the way to receive faith.

> But which of you, having a servant plowing or feeding cattle, will say unto him by and by, when he is come from the field, Go and sit down to meat? And will not rather say unto him, Make ready wherewith I may sup, and gird thyself, and serve me, till I have eaten and drunken; and afterward thou shalt eat and drink? Doth he thank that servant because he did the things that were commanded him? I trow not. So likewise ye, when ye shall have done all those things which are commanded you, say, We are unprofitable servants: we have done that which was our duty to do (17:7–10 [KJV]).

---

2. Penington, *Works*, 1:239–40.

Jesus is telling his disciples to attend to the work that is set before them and not to get ahead of themselves. As is often the case, Jesus uses rhetoric to make his point. Notice the shift in point of view in this passage indicated by the use of different pronouns: first, Jesus puts the disciples in the position of master ("But which of *you*, having a servant"); second, the pronoun shifts from the second to the third person, and the master is referred as "he," no longer as "you" ("Doth *he* thank that servant"); and third, Jesus moves to the first person pronoun "we," thus putting the disciples in the position not of the master, nor the onlooker, but of the servant ("say, *We* are unprofitable servants"). Jesus has gently moved the disciples to seeing themselves as servants rather than seeing themselves as masters, the latter being their natural inclination. Faith is the hearing/obeying relationship with our Creator, and we are not our own masters, though we have claimed to be so since the Fall.

We are to serve righteousness, whether instructed by the conscience or later by the law of faith to serve THE LORD OUR RIGHTEOUSNESS (Jer 23:6 [KJV]); that is our duty. That duty will vary from person to person, but the rigorous standard of adhering to what is true and right does not vary from person to person. That standard is righteousness, and the soul must hunger and thirst after it, that it may be filled with faith. It is the sincerity of pursuit that is judged by Christ. We cannot obtain righteousness ourselves, any more than we can judge ourselves; we are subject to judgment. We, however, can and must do, like the servants in this parable, "all those things which are commanded" to us, laboring inoffensively and honestly that we may in faith come to cease from our own works.

> For he that is entered into his rest, he also hath ceased from his own works, as God did from his. Let us labour therefore to enter into that rest, lest any man fall after the same example of unbelief. For the word of God is quick, and powerful, and sharper than any twoedged sword, piercing even to the dividing asunder of soul and spirit, and of the joints and marrow, and is a discerner of the thoughts and intents of the heart. Neither is there any creature that is not manifest in his sight: but all things are naked and opened unto the eyes of him with whom we have to do (Heb 4:10-13 [KJV]).

His Seed Remaineth

As I wrote in the essay "Increase Our Faith," having faith, [a person] can thrive even when planted in the chaos of the world that lies in wickedness, even as a sycamine tree could be planted in a hostile environment of the sea.[1] Having faith, the hearing/obeying relationship with his Creator, man is restored, strengthened, and empowered to withstand and rise above such assaults upon his soul. He is given the power of God to rule over his human nature and to thrive regardless of the circumstances.

Half a dozen years ago, I was walking with a friend on the Haverford College campus, which is in a suburb of Philadelphia, Pennsylvania. It was the beginning of the school year, and some students—about thirty—had gathered on the college lawn to play a game that I'd never seen before. Intrigued, I suggested to my friend that we take a moment to watch the progress of the game. I recall her saying that the game was called "Zombie Tag," and it began with a few students walking stiffly with arms outstretched among all the others, whose goal was to escape being tagged by them. When tagged, however, each victim also began to stalk others in a like manner—stiffly walking with arms outstretched. It surprised me to see how quickly the game progressed. As their number increased, the "walking dead" overcame "the living ones," and when all players had joined the ranks of "the undead," the game was over.

Being a gospel minister and regularly seeing in everyday events analogies to the life of the Spirit, it occurred to me that the game modelled some spiritual dynamics: humankind can be alive in the flesh yet dead in the Spirit (just like zombies!) and in both the game and real life, the walking death spreads by contact between one person and another. In the game, it is simple tagging, but in life, the spiritual contagion is spread by deceitful,

---

1. Luke 17:6 (King James Version; all subsequent citations are from this version).

unjust behavior perpetrated upon innocent victims, who then, in turn, become perpetrators, and on and on it goes.

The game did not mimic life, however, in one very significant way: whereas the game ends when all are caught and have become "zombies"; in real life, the death and darkness that consume need not be final: not all remain captive to the demonic forces that entice away life.

The good news is that while yet on earth and yet in time, we can receive life that is not subject to death, i.e., eternal life and the indwelling seed that keeps us from succumbing to the evil that men inflict upon their neighbors, and upon their brothers, as did that first perpetrator, Cain. ("And wherefore slew he him [Abel]? Because his own works were evil, and his brother's righteous" [1 John 3:12].)

For not only was Jesus sent to raise up humankind above the throes and threat of spiritual darkness and death, but he is now sent to retrieve us into and sustain us in his own unassailable state, where he—and thus we—have power over the living death and living hell.

> I am he that liveth, and was dead; and, behold, I am alive for evermore, Amen; and have the keys of hell and of death (Rev 1:18).

In the great prayer found in John 17 and expressed shortly before his execution, Jesus asks God to keep his disciples from the evil (15). Jesus was not asking that his disciples be removed from the trajectory of evil released by the animus of others, for ill-treatment comes to everyone in this world, and—as Jesus knows—those who "are not of the world" (John 15:19) will be targeted assiduously by the prince of the world through those who have come unwittingly to do his bidding.

In asking that his disciples be kept from the evil, Jesus is asking that the inward condition of their souls be kept inviolate and uncorrupted by the evil that will—without question—assault them. It is the soul's condition for which Jesus prays: that nothing in his disciples give foothold to "the prince of the power of the air" (Eph 2:2); i.e., that his disciples heed no temptation, that they forfeit no blessedness.

> The light of the body is the eye: if therefore thine eye be single, thy whole body shall be full of light (Matt 6:22).

Through singleness of mind, purity of heart, and focused obedience do his disciples overcome distraction and temptation. The physical sensation of being indwelled by the Spirit—the body full of light—is more than metaphor; it is actual sensation arising from the blessed integration of one's entire being: body and soul. It is the perfection of Christ's joy fulfilled in those who have been born of God, and do not commit sin, for his seed remains in them.

> Whosoever is born of God doth not commit sin; for his seed remaineth in him: and he cannot sin, because he is born of God. In this the children of God are manifest, and the children of the devil: whosoever doeth not righteousness is not of God, neither he that loveth not his brother (1 John 3:9–10).

The Solitary Ascent

Jesus saith unto her, Touch me not; for I am not yet ascended to my Father. . . . Then saith he to Thomas, Reach hither thy finger, and behold my hands; and reach hither thy hand, and thrust it into my side (John 20:17a, 27a).

JUST TEN VERSES SEPARATE these seemingly contradictory instructions about touch that Jesus gives to these two followers: first, he cautions Mary *not* to touch him, and a short while later, he urges Thomas not only to touch him but to do so invasively: to feel his wounds. Clearly, there's a difference in the significance given to "touch" in these two stories.

In the second instance, touch is the means by which the unbelieving Thomas is convinced of the reality that death has occurred and is followed by resurrection to life. Here touch stands for personal experience that precipitates convincement. Sensory perception—the feeling, seeing, hearing—is a type or shadow for the inward perception of the substance. That substance is accessible only through the eye of faith, which alone senses and convinces of the reality of the lordship of Christ. ("And Thomas answered and said unto him, My Lord and my God" [20:28].) In this episode Thomas and the other disciples learn that their work will be to convince others of the Truth through bestirring an inward apprehension, which sensory perception approximates.

In the first story, Mary has just recognized the Lord and has lovingly reached toward him; here touch has a different function and significance. Jesus is not teaching or convincing or engaged in any outwardly directed assistance to others, as he later would be in his encounter with Thomas and the disciples; rather he is here concerned with protecting himself and his intent to ascend to the Father.

He had been delivered into the earth but a few days before: killed and entombed; he had now risen out of the earth and was walking upon it; and, to complete his course, he was to rise above the earth to "sitteth on the right hand of God" (Col 3:1). He would, therefore, not be deterred by worldly attachment here symbolized by touch. In this exchange with the woman, touch stands for an intimacy that can derail the soul in her journey upward toward completion, perfection, i.e., the soul's ascent into heaven. Jesus confirms this fact when he keeps Mary at arm's length by explaining; "for I am not yet ascended to my Father."

The imagery of being first held under and then subsequently rising out of the earth can be seen frequently in early Friends writings. (Italics are mine.)

> [S]hake yourselves from *the dust of the earth* and come away in faithfulness and obedience to your call. —J. Fothergill
>
> [Y]our minds will be animated and *lifted up above the world* and the fading, perishing things of it. —T. Scattergood
>
> Must not they who are . . . free from the world through the cross of Christ, the power of God . . . walk as freemen, *having the earth under them and not over them?* —W. Edmundson [1]

In George Fox's vision of 1671, the same earth-as-encumbrance imagery occurs, but here it is applied en masse, perhaps an indication of Fox's realization of the universality of the earthly, darkened condition in which humanity lies spiritually dead and buried, as well as of his life's work to turn people—in large numbers—from darkness to light. He tells us:

> And I had a vision about the time that I was in this travail and sufferings, that I was walking in the fields and many Friends were with me, and I bid them dig in the earth, and they did and I went down. And there was a mighty vault top-full of people kept under the earth, rocks, and stones. So I bid them break open the earth and let all the people out, and they did, and all the people came forth to liberty; and it was a mighty place. And when they had done I went on and bid them dig again. They did, and there was a mighty vault full of people, and I bid them throw it down and let all the people out, and so they did.[2]

---

1. *Epigraph.* John 20:17a, 27a (King James Version; all subsequent citations are from this version). MSF, *Path*, Aug. 18–21, 2019.

2. Nickalls, *Journal*, 578.

As earlier illustrated in the chapter from John, Jesus—while in progress from earth to heaven—addressed two concerns: (1) his work of convincing/liberating others, and (2) protecting himself from earthly attachment. In this vision of Fox, we see these same two concerns likewise acknowledged, and yes, touch—signifying attachment—is again the metaphor, and the woman—signifying the earthly—is again the threat. Fox's vision continues:

> And I went on again and bid them dig again, and Friends said unto me, "George, thou finds out all things," and so there they digged, and I went down, and went along the vault; and there sat a woman in white looking at time how it passed away. And there followed me a woman down in the vault, in which vault was the treasure; and so she laid her hand on the treasure on my left hand and then time whisked on apace; but I clapped my hand upon her and said, "Touch not the treasure." And then time passed not so swift.[3]

A closer look at the particulars of this passage is worth taking. Fox is journeying down into the earth; he is discovering what in his own nature is to be found that is susceptible to earthly encumbrance. He is not here focused on his work to convince/liberate captivated humanity. Rather, here he searches out what threatens to captivate himself: and thus, he must descend into his own earthly, underground dynamics of being.

There are two women in this vision, which function to alert one that no particular woman is meant here; rather that "woman" as category is intended (and we extend the boundary of that category to encompass "the opposite sex"). This same rhetorical device is used in chapter 11 of Revelation where "two witnesses" do not signify particular witnesses but instead stand for the category of "those who witness," that, as a type, they may be informed of their role and expectations, which are listed in that chapter.

The first woman Fox envisions is seated, dressed in white, and "looking at time." Interpreted, the woman is seated and at rest; she's among those "which came out of great tribulation, and have washed their robes, and made them white in the blood of the Lamb" (Rev 7:14). She looks at time, which interpreted is to say, she is not in time but is apart from it and observing it; she is where there is "time no longer" (Rev 10:6), i.e., she knows life eternal. In this first woman, we learn what qualities pertain to the person who potentially poses a threat to the prophet's sensibility: one who is spiritually cognizant.

3. Nickalls, *Journal*, 578.

Fox moves on, followed by the second woman, deeper into the earth, and we see, envisioned in dream-like imagery, both the threat and the action taken to thwart it. In the second vault, "the treasure" lay, which I interpret to mean, the place where was found his sense of life. It is his left hand that is touched—not the hand with which he labors, but that part of his being not given to his work; it is there the claim upon him is made: to engage that which is not his work but some other genuine, vital part of his being, for example, his emotion. We are told time moves rapidly as a consequence, which indicates a waste of resources (time, effort, attention, etc.) that follows the misdirection of attention toward a personal, nonproductive area of life. Closely replicating Jesus's words to Mary, Fox resists this claim upon himself, saying: "Touch not the treasure." We then see "time passed not so swift," which is interpreted to mean, he no longer saw his resources wasted.

Perhaps it was the personal, non-work directed nature of the topic that led Fox to conclude this journal entry with cryptic words, hinting he could speak more to the point if he chose but would instead leave interpretation to another.

> They that can read these things must have the earthy, stony nature off them. And see how the stones and the earth came upon man since the beginning, since he fell from the image of God and righteousness and holiness. And much I could speak of these things, but I leave them to the right eye and reader to see and read.[4]

In the first verse of the Epistle to the Romans, Paul describes himself as "separated unto the gospel of God." In his exegetical work of the same name, Karl Barth expands upon the phrase:

> Paul . . . is always himself, and moves essentially on the same plane as all other men. But, in contradiction to himself and in distinction from all others, he is—called by God and sent forth. Are we then to name him a Pharisee? Yes, a Pharisee—"separated," isolated, and distinct. But he is a Pharisee of a higher order. Fashioned of the same stuff as all other men, a stone differing in no way from other stones, yet in his relation to God—and in this only—he is unique. As an apostle—and only as an apostle—he stands in no organic relationship with human society as it exists in history; seen from the point of view of human society, he can be regarded only as an exception, nay, rather, as an impossibility. Paul's position can be justified only as resting in God, and so only can his

---

4. Nickalls, *Journal*, 578.

words be regarded as at all credible, for they are as incapable of direct apprehension as is God Himself. For this reason he dares to approach others and to demand a hearing without fear either of exalting himself or of approximating too closely to his audience. He appeals only to the authority of God. This is the ground of his authority. There is no other.[5]

"Separated, isolated, and distinct," and not "approximating too closely" with those to whom he ministers is the platform from which this apostle must work; as must the prophet, Fox; and even the Messiah himself. Barth states that only thus could Paul retain "the ground of his authority": that "his words [could] be regarded as at all credible." In each of these three instances—whether with Jesus, Paul, or Fox—the work entails a resistance to an "organic relationship with human society."

What was present in the two earlier illustrations but absent from Barth's analysis, however, is the more foundational motive: In addition to ensuring the viability of one's mission and work in the vineyard of God, there is the elemental drive to secure the soul's solitary, heavenward ascent; one must "go it alone."

---

5. Barth, *Romans*, 27–28.

Powers of the Soul

We should use the three aspects of the soul fittingly and in accordance with nature, as created by God. We should use our incensive power against our outer self and against Satan. "Be incensed," it is written, "against sin" (Ps 4:4), that is, be incensed with yourselves and the devil, so that you will not sin against God. Our desire should be directed towards God and towards holiness. Our intelligence should control our incensive power and our desire with wisdom and skill, regulating them, admonishing them, correcting them and ruling them as a king rules over his subjects.—*The Philokalia*

THE PHILOKALIA IS A collection of texts by spiritual masters of the Eastern Orthodox Church hesychast tradition. The texts were written between the fourth and fifteenth centuries for the guidance and instruction of monks who undertook contemplative life. The Greek word "philokalia" comprises two separate words, which together signify love of the beautiful and the good.

In *The Philokalia*, the writers are agreed that the soul has three distinct aspects or powers: the appetitive, the incensive, and the intellect. (Greek Christian Fathers accepted this three-part formulation that originated with Plato.) The first two powers can be used naturally to one's benefit, or unnaturally to one's disadvantage. Using these powers naturally and beneficially prepares one to receive Christ. Unnatural use is the result of having been overcome by demons that adulterate these God-bestowed powers, and thus prevent those whom they corrupt from preparing themselves to receive Christ.

For example, the appetitive power is used naturally and beneficially when one loves and desires to know God with all one's heart, or—for the yet unredeemed—when one loves the beautiful and the good. And conversely, the appetitive power is used unnaturally when one is driven by desires for worldly gain or sensory pleasures: for example, the desire that leads a person to crave admiration or to become gluttonous.

The soul's incensive power is misused when it is directed toward those who interfere with one's desire or conceit. This misuse is experienced as anger or rancor toward another whom one holds responsible for one's discontent, having had one's desire or conceit thwarted. Naturally and beneficially, the incensive power can be used to intensify one's longing for God or to ward off demonic anger towards others. By relying on the intellect to redirect that anger, the intensive power turns against and expels the demons who've infiltrated the soul, and thus obstructed unity with Christ.

The intellect is the power that guides the appetitive and incensive powers. When it is exercised well, the intellect directs the two other powers away from the temptation to yield to demonic influence. If the intellect's power is not exercised well, the person becomes unaware of his own sin—as if spiritually blind or asleep—and becomes corrupt. (In Quaker parlance, his conscience is "seared.")

When one is targeted by a corrupt person who discharges cruelty and deceit, one can become distracted from the primal duty to maintain purity of heart, and instead resort to blaming the sinful other for one's own distress. A way of dealing with this temptation to blame others (which is a misuse of the incensive power) is to avoid the temptation altogether by setting a hedge between one's soul and whatever offends. That is to say, one can create a space wherein one more easily realizes one's intent to receive Christ. By simply preventing extraneous threats from the demonic—as given conduit by others—one eliminates interference with one's readiness to receive Christ. For this reason, the practice of withdrawing from the world has long been a monastic and hermitic practice.

Employing such a barrier against the world is an ascetic technique to foster growth (as is the general intent of *The Philokalia*); it is not, however, the state of wholeness or perfection to which we are called, and likewise find heralded in early Friends' writings. Faith does not simply avoid the maligned but acts (when directed by Christ) to confront and overcome evil by speaking truth. Such maturity of faith is known only as one receives the power of God that overcomes the world, as Christ Jesus affirms when he states: "In the world ye shall have tribulation: but be of good cheer; I have overcome the world."[1]

This aim is aspired to when one strongly loves and desires God (and for the unredeemed: when one loves and desires the beautiful and the good) so that one's attention and heart are purified through willing one thing (Matt 5:8). Then is the intellect rightly used, the other powers of the soul well-ordered, and the soul prepared to receive Christ. In Christ, we are fully empowered to repel demonic infiltration of the soul, and to expel all sin. Through Christ, our savior, the demons are cast out, and we become perfect; our faith makes us whole. In a world that lies in wickedness (1 John 5:19) and ignorance, Christ, the power of God, is the only power stronger than the demonic.

It is better to see the sin of the world as uniform and single rather than to view its manifestations as particular properties belonging to specific corrupted persons. That is to say, in its uniformity, the world's sin is more like an expanse of mud than it is like separate rocks situated at intervals in a field! Seeing sin as a uniform force helps the intellect direct the incensive power toward sin itself, and away from particular offenders who have succumbed to and embody demonic power.

It is written that Jesus took on and overcame the sin of the world. It is germane to this statement that sin be considered a cohesive, single condition rather than a variety of particular disorders or deeds, each being the property or possession of individual persons, which is a psychological idea. Entertaining the prevailing modern notion of individual autonomy, one may be averse to yielding the claim of the self's possessive power, even when that possession pertains to disorders of the self! It is a turnaround to accept that it is not people who possess sin but are, in fact, possessed by sin.

The older, biblical understanding allows one to see the world's wickedness differently, and to replace the all-too-human response of resentment or anger towards the corrupt with a response of merciful pity and concern, as did our savior, "who knew what was in man" (John 2:25). In unity with Christ Jesus, we overcome that which is in man; through Christ, we overcome the world.

> And if I go and prepare a place for you, I will come again, and receive you unto myself; that where I am, there ye may be also (John 14:3).

1. *Epigraph.* Palmer et al. *Philokalia*, 1:184. John 16:33 (King James Version; all subsequent citations are from this version).

Enduring unto the End

If we died with him, we shall live with him;
    if we endure, we shall reign with him.
If we deny him, he will deny us.
If we are faithless, he keeps faith,
    for he cannot deny himself (2 Tim 2:11–13).

THESE SIMPLE, BEAUTIFUL LINES are preceded by the Apostle's guarantee: "Here are words you may trust." It seems likely that he's informing us that the words are inspired, and therefore trustworthy. In addition, the breadth and depth of understanding, expressed in so few words, is indicative of inspired authorship. So few words to speak of such a lengthy process, for the dying mentioned in the first line is slow and difficult and, as a result, widely avoided. Nevertheless, the long, inward process is laid out for us in the Scriptures' apocalyptic passages; there we're given words about what to expect: where we are going and who will come to us in the end.

    Each synoptic gospel contains an apocalyptic chapter; I prefer the one in the book of Mark because the language is concise, intense, and powerful. Chapter 13 begins with Jesus providing his disciples with an image and prediction of a destroyed temple. The disciples had been impressed with the buildings of their religion and said so, but Jesus tells them that "all will be thrown down" (Mark 13:2 [NEB]). Though he speaks of the culture's dwelling space for God, he is referring to the inward dwelling place of *our* human spirits: our religious, philosophical, psychological, and cultural concepts in which we posit our understanding of self and world. These, Jesus says, will be thrown down.

    Many of the chapter's subsequent verses (13:7–20) describe destruction, turmoil, and distress: war, earthquakes, famine, betrayals, upheavals, family disruption, and fleeing one's home and land. The significance of this imagery is two-fold: (1) in one form or another, life's distresses will be the lot of all, and (2) this is not chosen but visited upon us, and endured. Personal trials are unique yet come universally to us all. It is as if Jesus, using poetic images, is giving an overview of life's calamities: specific calamities that when conjointly listed imply the universality of loss and affliction.

This onslaught over time will, in truth, undermine confidence in all existential concepts, even those concepts of "self," "God," and "love"; this is one's own personal inward suffering "such as never has been until now since the beginning of the world which God created" (13:19 [NEB]). Jesus tells us how we're to handle it: we're to endure unto the end.[1] To endure is to hold to the deep, wordless human insistence that truth must be honored, though it shakes to the ground every manmade notion of earth and heaven and leaves one feeling lost, without bearings. Such endurance during the temptation to despair is the material of Quaker journal writings and the experience of all true Christians.

Knowing the extreme suffering and despair of the inward process, the cross within, Jesus warns us upfront to not be deceived and misled by those who come saying that they are the light of Christ:

> Jesus began: "Take care that no one misleads you. Many will come claiming my name, and saying, 'I am he'; and many will be misled by them" (13:5–6 [NEB]).

By making grand claims for themselves, such persons will mislead and foment a symbiotic relationship with any whose endurance has flagged and are ready to forfeit. A primary tactic of such is to manipulate by flattery, appealing to the ego of the willing victim by suggesting he's already knowledgeable of God: in Paul's words "saying that [his] resurrection has already taken place (2 Tim 2:18 [NEB]). Second, any check on this corrupt teaching will be denigrated as unworthy, thereby eliminating any standard for exposing the false gospel. The willing participant, in return, offers tribute in the form of loyalty and support, for he thinks himself released from his responsibility to endure, as Jesus has called him to do. This alliance upsets people's faith, and so Jesus prominently places his warning against it at the start of his discourse. Early Friends admonished this dynamic when they

---

1. *Epigraph.* 2 Tim 2:11–13 (The New English Bible [NEB]). Mark 13:13b (King James Version [KJV]).

saw it by recalling the prophet's words: "the priests bear rule by their means; and my people love to have it so" (Jer 5:31 [KJV]).

The Son of man comes inwardly to those who endure "unto the end, [for] the same shall be saved" (Mark 13:13 [KJV]). Salvation is known by the inward coming of the Lord, "then shall they see the Son of man coming in the clouds with great power and glory" (Mark 13:26 [KJV]); *his coming is known by the complete otherness of his person, for he is a person, neither solely a principle nor an essence.* The coming of the Son of man is that which no person can effect by his own desire or aspiration or sacrifice; the coming of the Lord is out of our hands entirely, Jesus teaches. We do not know how to turn to the Son of man because we have no idea what he is inwardly, what to expect; his coming will not resemble in the slightest our human concepts of light and love, or even our concepts of God. We know neither the substance nor the timing of this inward event: "But about that day or that hour no one knows, not even the angels in heaven, not even the Son; only the Father" (13:32 [NEB]). It is entirely other, for our deliverance is the prerogative of our Creator, not of our creaturely aspiration.

We can reject this ancient wisdom of our tradition but do so at our peril: "Heaven and earth shall pass away: but my words will shall not pass away" (13:31 [KJV]). A faithless turn to idolatry only destroys one's chances of salvation; it in no way impacts the soteriological structure by which we are called to abide: endurance in the truth until the end.

> If we are faithless, he keeps faith, for he cannot deny himself (2 Tim 2:13 [NEB]).

Opening the Scriptures
Parable of the Wheat and the Tares

He that soweth the good seed is the Son of man; The field is the world; the good seed are the children of the kingdom; but the tares are the children of the wicked one; The enemy that sowed them is the devil; the harvest is the end of the world; and the reapers are the angels. As therefore the tares are gathered and burned in the fire; so shall it be in the end of this world. The Son of man shall send forth his angels, and they shall gather out of his kingdom all things that offend, and them which do iniquity; And shall cast them into a furnace of fire: there shall be wailing and gnashing of teeth. Then shall the righteous shine forth as the sun in the kingdom of their Father. Who hath ears to hear, let him hear (Matt 13:37–43).

JESUS IS HERE PRIVATELY explaining to his disciples the parable of the wheat and the tares (Matt 13:24–30), one of the stories he had given to the multitude a short time before. The parable itself, as well as Jesus's explanation of it, is usually interpreted in the following way: those people who are good will go to heaven when they die, and those who are bad will be thrust into hell.

It's a comforting affirmation for those who consider themselves righteous: in the by-and-by, all will receive their just deserts. Furthermore, such an interpretation quiets the urge to take matters into one's own hands: to wreak justice as spiritual vigilante, punishing wrongdoers who have disturbed one's well-being, or egotistic self-regard.

Through the ages, this particular interpretation of the parable has likely saved many from abuse, and some of them—perhaps in greater proportion to their number—were prophets. As well as safeguarding would-be victims from the misguided and malicious, this interpretation may also have benefited potential perpetrators, restraining hubris from descending into action.

Although it's had its beneficial uses, this interpretation of the parable of the wheat and the tares is not the one that George Fox presents to us. Fox sees from a different perspective and therefore arrives at a different interpretation. We can study his interpretation of this parable because Fox reveals it in his third epistle. Here is the sum total of that short epistle:

> Friends,—There is an eye, that hath looked to see the good seed, that was sown, and queried, from whence came these tares? The answer was and is; "The wicked one hath sown them." Now read the tares, and what is the effect of them, and their work? And what they do, and have done? How they hang amongst the wheat? But now is the time of harvest, that both wheat and tares are seen, and each distinguished, the one from the other.[1]

To understand Fox's perspective, one begins by isolating his own words from those which are found in the original Bible passage. His own words indicate his interpretation of the text. For example, the epistle's first sentence is "There is an eye": no such reference to this "eye" occurs in the text of the parable; it is strictly Fox's expression. In communicating his first response to the parable by referring to "an eye," Fox asserts the parable is about seeing; it is about seeing or knowing the difference between good and evil (good seed or evil tares). With that much information given, we know that Fox is relating the parable to the Fall, for to "know[ing] good and evil" (Gen 3:5) independent from God's guidance was the temptation offered by the Serpent. In taking that bait—to no longer eye God's Will—humanity became spiritually blind, unable to see, to discern good from evil. The "eye" Fox refers to is that which has overcome that blindness by again eyeing God; this "eye" sees: "both the wheat and tares are seen, and each distinguished, the one from the other."[2]

That the "eye" is but one eye—and not the two eyes given by nature—implies a special kind of seeing, the seeing that metaphorically refers to understanding, or insight. Fox refers to seeing "the good" and the evil that exist within each unredeemed human: "[the tares] hang amongst the wheat."

---

1. *Epigraph.* Matt 13:37–43 (King James Version; all subsequent biblical citations are from this version). Fox, *Works*, 7:17–18.

2. Fox, *Works*, 7:18.

For Fox, the parable is first a lesson on spiritual discernment: seeing, and second, a lesson on what one sees: evil is within oneself; with surprise, one asks: "from whence came these tares?"[3]

Fox urges an examination of the evil that grows within. ("Now read the tares"; that is to say, now that you see the evil in yourself, learn about it.) He directs the reader to examine the characteristics and consequences of that inward evil: "[W]hat is the effect of [the tares], and their work? And what they do, and have done? How they hang amongst the wheat?"[4]

Fox is compelling the reader to see the effects of sin and wrongdoing in his life, and the stubborn persistence of sin in human nature, as tares "hang amongst the wheat." For to see—to sense—the distinction between good and evil, and the harm evil does to oneself and others, is the first step to knowing "to refuse the evil, and choose the good" (Isa 7:15).

The "harvest," a word found in both the original text and Fox's epistle, does not refer to physical death, and neither does it refer to some cataclysmic end of all life on earth, as is often portrayed in non-Quaker interpretations. These wrong interpretations result from assigning a literal meaning to Jesus's words: "the harvest is the end of the world" (Matt 13:39).

For Fox, the end of the world is the end of the worldly self, the unredeemed, fallen self that is in opposition to and independent of God. Dying to that self, the inward cross, is the worldly death that entails "wailing and gnashing of teeth" (Matt 13:42). Once this inward separation of spirit from worldly flesh, wheat from tares, good from evil, has taken place, and the tares gathered and burned, "[t]hen," says Jesus, "shall the righteous shine forth as the sun in the kingdom of their Father. Who hath ears to hear, let him hear" (Matt 13:43).

Jesus's final statement ("Who hath ears to hear, let him hear.") informs us that not all will grasp his meaning. He and other prophets realize comprehension comes only when the mysteries of the kingdom are unveiled by the Holy Ghost (John 14:26). In his address to London Yearly Meeting in 1675, Fox identified the parables, however, as one tool that prepares humankind to receive the Holy Ghost: "Here is the bundle of life opened, the end of the parables, and of the figures, and law, and who fulfilleth it."[5]

When Jesus's disciples asked him why he spoke in parables, he said:

---

3. Fox, *Works*, 7:17.
4. Fox, *Works*, 7:17–18.
5. Skinner and Stillwell, *That Thy Candles*, 107.

> Because it is given unto you to know the mysteries of the kingdom of heaven, but to them it is not given. . . . Therefore speak I to them in parables: because they seeing see not; and hearing they hear not, neither do they understand. And in them is fulfilled the prophecy of Esaias, which saith, By hearing ye shall hear, and shall not understand; and seeing ye shall see, and shall not perceive: For this people's heart is waxed gross and their ears are dull of hearing, and their eyes they have closed; lest at any time they should see with their eyes and hear with their ears, and should understand with their heart, and should be converted, and I should heal them (Matt 13:11–15).

As did the prophets before them, seventeenth-century Friends understood that the worldly nature (described in this excerpt where Jesus quotes Isaiah [Isa 6:10]) could not understand the Scriptures. It is "by the inward testimony of the Spirit we do alone truly know [the Scriptures]," wrote Barclay.[6] No amount of scholarship, knowledge of Hebrew or Greek, nor seminary training could explicate the words given through the spirit of prophecy. The same dependency on the Spirit is required to understand early Friends' writings: no amount of reading, training, or knowledge of history or doctrine can open the meaning of their writings. Because they are written from the spirit of Truth, they must be read in that same spirit.

> For I saw in that light and spirit which was before the scriptures were given forth, and which led the holy men of God to give them forth, that all must come to that spirit, if they would know God or Christ, or the scriptures aright, which they that gave them forth were led and taught by.[7]

Fox here confirms the Scripture message that all must come to that Spirit (Rev 22:17), if they would understand the words of the prophets and apostles that have come before. It is this Spirit of Christ that enables us to understand the writings of these prophetic men and women, regardless of the century in which they wrote—first, seventeenth, in between, or after—and to discern the spirit of Truth from the spirit of error: to distinguish the wheat from the tares.

> Ye are of God, little children, and have overcome them: because greater is he that is in you, than he that is in the world. They are of the world: therefore speak they of the world, and the world

---

6. Barclay, *Apology*, 62.
7. Fox, *Works*, 1:89.

heareth them. We are of God: he that knoweth God heareth us; he that is not of God heareth not us. Hereby know we the spirit of truth, and the spirit of error (1 John 4:4–6).

Shooting the Moon
An Essay on Reflection and Substance

ONE SATURDAY EACH MONTH, Friends from around the Philadelphia area meet at a specified meetinghouse for what is called "Extended Worship." The schedule for the day is worship for several hours in the morning, then lunch and gathering in the afternoon for an opportunity to share one's response to the morning's ministry, or the insights silently gained during worship. The event usually draws around a dozen or so Friends, and, for the most part, it has settled into a gathering of regular attenders, of which I am one.

Another regular attender, whom I'll refer to as "S," has been struggling with cancer for a while, and her messages often bring forth some of what that struggle entails: the fear, confusion, sense of loss, the desire for healing, and the striving to remain hopeful. That morning her message came to us as a story of a recent experience she'd had while hospitalized and interacting with other patients and their families in the waiting room of a twelfth-floor oncology ward.

"S" is an artist, and for some time, it's been her practice to photograph the full moon each month. In her message, she described other times she'd photographed the moon: times when the light of evening was just right; the sky a clear, warm blue in the moments before dark; and times when the moon was tinged with the reflected light of the setting sun. Having a twelfth-floor vantage point overlooking Philadelphia, she saw a unique opportunity to photograph the moon as it rose above the horizon and was mirrored in the towering, glass-walled buildings of the city.

Her camera, tripod, and other equipment brought in by a friend, "S" prepared to get the shot, as interested onlookers joined in the fun of sharing her quest. The waiting room began to hum with curiosity, talk, and laughter as other patients; their kids, parents, and grandparents; friends; and staff chatted and hoped the cloud cover might break and the moon appear, which in the end, it did.

The primary cause for joy for those in the room, however, was not the successful completion of the quest, but the warm person-to-person interaction that had emerged. The group found among themselves, at least for a time, the wherewithal to withstand and overcome the fear of impending threat and loss. Just as the rising moon may reflect the sun's rays, we humans can also glow in the beauty of our nature. When her message finished, this hymn came to mind:

> For the beauty of the earth / And the glory of the skies,
> For the love which from our birth / Over and around us lies.
> Lord of all to thee we raise / This our hymn of grateful praise.[1]

Sitting in the silence that followed, appreciating the richness of the story and the liveliness it depicted, I thought that God is glorified in his creatures when we act with courage and ability, with creativity and warmth, and with love.

Then unexpectedly Jesus's words from John 17 appeared in my mind: "Father . . . glorify thy Son, that thy Son also may glorify thee."[2] These words begin the prayer Jesus gives just before his arrest, which leads to the events that he knows will bring an end to his earthly life. As the verse presented such an abrupt alternative to what I had been feeling and thinking, I realized I needed to examine the passage.

> Father, the hour is come; glorify thy Son, that thy Son also may glorify thee: As thou hast given him power over all flesh, that he should give eternal life to as many as thou hast given him (John 17:1–2).

Jesus begins the prayer by acknowledging that God is the source of life: he addresses him as "Father"; he appeals to Him for power to complete his mission, a mission that God has given. Jesus's initial words express a dependency on God for purpose, strength, and love. Here there are no mediating activities or relationships; instead there is a direct one-to-one interaction between the Creator and the human being, a reciprocality: Jesus, as man, is to be glorified through receiving God's presence, and God is to be glorified by Jesus's conformity to his Will. It is a relationship that retains the

---

1. Pierpoint, *Methodist Hymnal,* 35.
2. John 17:1 (King James Version; all subsequent citations are from this version).

distinction between Creator and creature, and yet interiorizes that relationship through the indwelling of God in man: "as thou, Father, art in me, and I in thee, that they also may be one in us" (17:21).

Secondly, in this passage, Jesus identifies his mission: he is to give others eternal life; he is not intent upon bettering the natural state by lessening fear, creating beauty, or by forming bonds of affection. His mission can proceed only upon his having received "power over all flesh," i.e., the power to withstand any claims made upon the will by the first nature that exists independent of God.

Given the circumstances, one might suppose that the impulse to self-preservation would figure in this prayer, but throughout, there is no sign of it. Jesus instead focuses on making known the glory he has been given, and in turn gives to others (17:22). In like manner for us, to know the glory received from Christ blinds us to every natural impulse; for there is neither seen nor felt a forfeiture or sense of loss to the first nature, as one receives and focuses upon the light of Christ within. Such is the complete power and beauty of our Lord, who is the Substance forevermore.

> In this stands our blessedness and everlasting happiness, as our eye is kept always looking to Jesus, the author and finisher of our faith, and not only to know him as the author the beginner of faith, but as the finisher and ender also, and to know the end of faith, which is the salvation of our souls.... Many are living witnesses in this age, as in ages past, of the power of faith, even in the beginning of its work. But it is a higher state to know the end of it, the finishing of faith, even to know its work done, to know the heart purified by it, and the victory over the world obtained, the wicked one subdued, overcome, brought down, and destroyed. This is a blessed state indeed, and that which all are to wait for, press after, and witness. The only way to attain this is to always look to Jesus, to keep the eye of the mind toward him, and the ear open to him, who alone teaches to profit, even in silence, when no word is spoken outwardly. This is the blessed end of the ministry and the ministers of truth whom the Lord has sent among us, and of all preaching, writing, and printing, even that everyone's eye might be turned to Jesus, always looking to him who has begun the good work, and who alone is able to finish it.[3]

---

3. Shewen, *Meditations*, 74–75.

As I Have Loved You

Whither I go, ye cannot come; so now I say to you. A new commandment I give unto you, That ye love one another; as I have loved you, that ye also love one another. By this shall all men know that ye are my disciples, if ye have love one to another. Simon Peter said unto him, Lord, whither goest thou? Jesus answered him, Whither I go, thou canst not follow me now; but thou shalt follow me afterwards. Peter said unto him, Lord, why cannot I follow thee now? I will lay down my life for thy sake. Jesus answered him, Wilt thou lay down thy life for my sake? Verily, verily, I say unto thee, The cock shall not crow, till thou hast denied me thrice (John 13:33b–38).

THE WORDS "AS I have loved you" stand out when I read this passage. They qualify the meaning of the new commandment that Jesus has given to his disciples: to love one another. Adding "as I have loved you" make this commandment different from the love that is naturally known in every human heart: love for kith and kin; love for those we admire; or love for those who provide for, participate with, or in any way please us. The words "as I have loved you" bring a new, different meaning to the word "love," and we can no longer let those feelings that we formerly called "love" occupy the prime position in our hearts. For what Jesus commands is not a human but a divine love, what Paul describes as the "love [that] has flooded our inmost heart through the Holy Spirit he [God] has given us."[1]

The contrast between the newly commanded love and the old human love is illustrated by Peter who expresses the human love that comes so naturally to us. Frequently in Scripture stories, Peter is the all-too-human

---

1. *Epigraph*. John 13:33b–38 (King James Version [KJV]). Rom 5:5 (The New English Bible [NEB]).

foil for the divine man Jesus. In this passage, Peter first reveals his lack of understanding: Where is Jesus going? Why can't he follow Jesus now? Then quick-on-the-heels comes Peter's avowal to the one he loves and admires: "I will lay down my life for thy sake" (John 13:37 [KJV]). Immediately Jesus puts this natural, deeply felt but ungrounded, human love in its rightful place: "The cock shall not crow, till thou hast denied me thrice" (13:38b [KJV]). Unlike the divine love that Jesus commands, the natural, human love is weak: contingent upon the needs, desires, powers, and fears of our human nature. Jesus commands us to love in a different way, a way which the natural human cannot grasp, cannot follow (John 13:33, 36), and so Jesus prepares the place for us (14:2–3 [KJV]).

The divine love that Jesus commands entails self-sacrifice, as does the love with which we're all familiar: our security or comfort gladly forfeited for the loved one's benefit. Peter's claim that he would lay down his life for Jesus's sake shows his willingness to sacrifice. Relying upon his own will, however, to carry through the sacrifice was Peter's error: human motivation rather than adherence to the divine law of love that Jesus commands. Peter's self-reliance on his own will and sentiment is, in fact, a form of self-exaltation, ironically dooming his intent from the outset: rather than sacrificing himself, he exalts himself believing in the strength of his feelings; he places faith in human power. When the cock crowed, Peter's crowing self-exaltation fell, along with his bitter tears (Matt 26:75 [KJV]). Peter typifies each of us when we put our faith in our own power to love others as he loved us.

When Jesus commands his disciples to love one another as he has loved them, *it is a command to know God*, for it is only in knowing God that we are in unity with him and his love. Our ability to love depends first upon knowing God, a dependence that can be seen in the answer given by Jesus when asked by a scribe for the first commandment:

> The first of all the commandments is, Hear, O Israel; The Lord our God is one Lord: And thou shalt love the Lord thy God with all thy heart, and with all thy soul, and with all thy mind, and with all thy strength: this is the first commandment. And the second is like, namely this, Thou shalt love thy neighbour as thyself (Mark 12:29–31a [KJV]).

The second is like the first commandment in that both are enacted by the power of God; in his image and likeness we feel and partake of his love for neighbor and for all, ourselves included.

The power of God's love is unchanging and not contingent upon the nature or behavior of the recipient. Unlike human love, no fear or resentment can impose upon or diminish it. In unity with God, as was Jesus, we too can love others free of the fear that giving our love will result in our loss or destruction.

> Ye have heard that it hath been said, Thou shalt love thy neighbour, and hate thine enemy. But I say unto you, Love your enemies, bless them that curse you, do good to them that hate you, and pray for them which despitefully use you, and persecute you; That ye may be children of your Father which is in heaven; for he maketh his sun to rise on the evil and on the good, and sendeth rain on the just and the unjust (Matt 5:43–45 [KJV]).

In knowing God and his love, we feel no such fear of loss from an enemy; our loss has already occurred and is swallowed up in abundant life.

When Jesus informs the disciples that he will prepare a place for them that they may follow him, he is speaking of the cross. In undergoing the cross, Jesus affirms that obedience to God, though entailing loss or even death, is preferable to all gratification gained through willful aspiration or enjoyed apart from God. In sacrificing himself on the cross in obedience to God's will, Jesus prepares a place for us: he shows the destruction of that which we call most inherent in human nature (knowledge from self) must precede the new heavenly being (wisdom) that will follow.

The new being, Christ, finds more happiness in knowing and obeying God than Adamic man gains through willfulness—or conforming to the will of the group, be it culture, folk, tribe, or congregation. The abundant joy in knowing God supersedes any sense of well-being known previously, all of which can be cast aside as no longer worthy of our desire. The completion we sought and pursued with such eager determination is now Given. That gift of faith is peerless as the pearl of great price.

All ancient religions see love as essential for happiness; only in Christianity does love become more than a virtue; it becomes a law, a commandment, which Jesus acknowledges, we cannot follow. It is the example that he has set for us that alerts us of something new, prepared, and waiting for us to come into: the knowledge of God and of his love.

> Beloved, let us love one another: for love is of God; and every one that loveth is born of God and knoweth God. He that loveth not, knoweth not God; for God is love (1 John 4:7–8 [KJV]).

Hear Ye Him
Some Observations on Matthew 17

And when they were come to Capernaum, they that received tribute money came to Peter, and said, Doth not your master pay tribute? He saith, Yes. And when he was come into the house, Jesus prevented him, saying, What thinkest thou, Simon? of whom do the kings of the earth take custom or tribute? of their own children, or of strangers? Peter saith unto him, Of strangers. Jesus saith unto him, Then are the children free. Notwithstanding, lest we should offend them, go thou to the sea, and cast an hook, and take up the fish that first cometh up; and when thou hast opened his mouth, thou shalt find a piece of money: that take, and give unto them for me and thee (Matt 17:24–27).

THIS ISN'T YOUR ORDINARY fish story, though it is incredible. Nevertheless, there's a lesson about reality being taught here: a lesson to be confirmed by experience alone. For the experience goes well beyond that which we have learned is possible in nature, just like the story itself.

Peter is being taught in this passage that the new way that Jesus embodies will free him from the confines of the first nature, the nature given to all humankind. The story conveys this lesson by transcending nature at large, i.e., by presenting a miracle. The story's miracle implies our human nature can likewise be transcended. By grace and truth, humankind's state can be moved beyond its corrupt, sinful nature into a new and living perfection.

Several other passages in this chapter affirm the real possibility of transcending our first-birth nature. When an idea is presented convincingly a number of times and in various ways, the likelihood of its being grasped is increased. One instance among the plethora of argument, evidence, and conviction may at last raise the veil that darkens the mind, plant a seed that grows in the heart.

> If ye have faith as a grain of mustard seed, ye shall say unto this mountain, Remove hence to yonder place; and it shall remove; and nothing shall be impossible unto you (17:20).[1]
> And they shall kill him, and the third day he shall be raised again (17:23).

Jesus's question to Peter ("of whom do the kings of the earth take custom or tribute? of their own children, or of strangers?" [17:25]) begins a course of reasoning designed to teach Peter that he has closer connection to God (as his child) than do those religious authorities who (alienated strangers to God) uphold religious, social regulations, such as paying and demanding tribute. Jesus is teaching Peter that he is beyond that alienated, tribute-paying nature of the world; he has a closer relationship to God: that of a son.

To finish his lesson with a demonstration of its truth, Jesus instructs Peter to perform an act that is impossible in nature: to get money from a fish's mouth. He has taught Peter that (human) nature can be transcended, and now he wants Peter himself to partake of this knowledge, to have it confirmed by experience. This passage is about coming into gospel freedom, freedom from captivity to corrupt human nature: the final line Jesus speaks to Peter before sending him off to find the fish is "[t]hen are the children free" (17:26).

There's a thematic symmetry in this chapter. The opening verses (1–5) also carry the lesson that with the coming of the new, living way, the paying of tribute is become defunct. In paying tribute—choosing what resources to give over to God—one assumes control and asserts this arrangement is just and adequate. In the new way that Jesus brings to the world, humankind no longer arbitrates the dispensing of resources to God, no longer pays tribute, but instead yields to God's command. Power and predominance of will shift their locus away from ourselves and onto God, once again to their rightful place that has been from the beginning.

> And after six days Jesus taketh Peter, James, and John his brother, and bringeth them up into an high mountain apart. And was transfigured before them: and his face did shine as the sun, and his

---

1. All citations are from the King James Version (KJV).

raiment was white as the light. And behold, there appeared unto them Moses and Elias talking with him. Then answered Peter, and said unto Jesus, Lord, it is good for us to be here: if thou wilt, let us make here three tabernacles; one for thee, and one for Moses, and one for Elias. While he yet spake, behold, a bright cloud overshadowed them; and behold a voice out of the cloud, which said, This is my beloved son, in whom I am well pleased; hear ye him (17:1–5).

We are told only of Peter's reaction to the appearance of Moses and Elias: he wants to honor them and Jesus—to pay tribute—by building tabernacles, one for each. (The tabernacle was a type or figure of God's dwelling with his people [Exod 25:8–9].) Even as Peter speaks of his intent to pay tribute, however, he is interrupted by the voice coming out of a bright cloud: "This is my beloved Son, in whom I am well pleased; hear ye him" (17:5). God's command, "hear ye him," disrupts Peter's plan. The voice commands the new way God is to dwell with his people: no longer through manmade tabernacles but by hearing the Word of God, which is Christ. The enveloping structure of the tabernacle is superseded by the enveloping cloud of light; paying tribute is superseded by hearing the beloved Son.

The middle passages of this chapter teach a variety of lessons about the work Peter and the other disciples will soon take up after Jesus has been killed. The timing, sequence, and history; the expectations of suffering and frustration; and the healings, their source, and how to perform them are all lessons covered in the middle section of the chapter. Yet standing like bookends at either end of the chapter is Jesus teaching the difference between the manmade religion of paying tribute, and the nature-transcending faith that comes down from above. The prominent position afforded this lesson in the first and last passages of this teaching chapter bespeak its significance as the first and last lesson that a disciple must learn.

The Inward Eclipse

ON AUGUST 21, 2017, there was a solar eclipse, and that day, these verses from Mark came to mind:

> But in those days, after that distress, the sun will be darkened, the moon will not give her light; the stars will come falling from the sky, the celestial powers will be shaken. Then they will see the Son of Man coming in the clouds with great power and glory, and he will send out the angels and gather his chosen from the four winds, from the farthest bounds of earth to the farthest bounds of heaven (Mark 13:24–27).

The words are from Jesus to his disciples. Prompted by their admiration of impressive temple (and temporal) buildings, Jesus informs them that "[n]ot one stone will be left upon another; all will be thrown down" (13:2 [NEB]). The theme throughout this discourse in Mark 13 is great destruction precedes the coming of the Lord, and Jesus drives the idea home with metaphor after metaphor.

Of course, as always, Jesus is talking about the inward condition/nature of human beings, not about the outward condition of nature. What is it that must be eclipsed within? What inward light of nature must be witnessed as dark futility, as death, before the new creation, the Son of Man, comes and replaces that old creation of human nature?

The truth of our limitations is bitter agony for us mortals, but choosing it over self-delusion leads to eternal life. It is the way, and when allowed daily to prevail, it will diminish us until the light of our nature—our hope and trust in our natural powers—is all but gone: "the celestial powers . . . shaken." It is not the end, but only the end of the alienated condition: our nature eclipsed by the coming of the Son of Man. "And what I say unto you, I say unto all. Watch."[1]

Watch the light of nature undergo the eclipse . . . within.

---

1. *Epigraph*. Mark 13:24–27 (The New English Bible [NEB]). Mark 13:37 (King James Version [KJV]).

Called to Christ

[THE FOLLOWING IS BASED upon vocal ministry given on October 1, 2017.]
In his journal, George Fox spoke of three kinds of dreams:

> For there were three sorts of dreams: for multitude of business sometimes caused dreams; and there were whisperings of Satan in man in the night-season; and there were speakings of God to man in dreams.[1]

In dreams we may learn something of ourselves that lies hidden during waking hours. The dream state allows access to a deeper awareness of who we are and what we think and feel. The self is not covered and veiled but revealed, and we can apply insights from dreams to better understand and improve our lives. We welcome this truth about ourselves and would like to always live with a deep awareness of truth, for there is freedom and comfort in it. Jesus said the truth makes us free, and he also said that the Comforter is the Spirit of Truth.[2] There is freedom and comfort in truth.

Fox also spoke of the two kinds of messages that the first Friends gave to people. To those who had not yet come into knowledge of God, Friends preached repentance. For repentance is an intentional uncovering of the truth about the self: what it is that must be seen and then laid down. In repentance, one chooses the light of truth over obscurity. The other kind of message that Friends preached was to those who had already gone through this coming into self-knowledge and had been given to see themselves as they were, without the Lord. They had been open to the truth of themselves and had discovered that the truth that is Christ soon after was revealed in them.

---

1. Nickalls, *Journal*, 9.
2. John 14:16–17 (KJV).

> To the world the apostles preached repentance, and to believe in Jesus Christ; and taught faith towards God. But to them who were redeemed out of the world, in whom the son of God was made manifest . . . preaching repentance and the doctrine of baptism was needless, in whom it was fulfilled, to and in such as were brought to God.[3]

They who saw themselves as they were without the Lord already knew the value of repentance, as it had led to their entry into the way, into the truth, and into the life that is Christ. They were free men and women who knew the Comforter, the Spirit of Truth. To these people, Friends preached Christ in them, because they were folks who sought to hear Christ, the Word, preached: it brought them to the living God; it was their life.

Fox writes: "There is a time of preaching faith towards God; and there is a time to be brought to God."[4] Whether we are in need of repentance or whether we are in the life of Christ, we are all human beings and must move forward from the position we are in. For it is to Christ that we are called: Christ in us the hope of glory.

---

3. Fox, *Works*, 7:143.
4. Fox, *Works*, 7:143.

Moses and the Burning Bush

[The following is based upon vocal ministry given on December 31, 2017.]

And the angel of the Lord appeared unto him in a flame of fire out of the midst of a bush: and he looked, and, behold, the bush burned with fire, and the bush was not consumed.[1]

ONE OF THE SIGNIFICANT things about the burning bush that Moses saw was that it continued to burn. The bush burned and was not consumed. And so, Moses was drawn to look at it: he'd not seen anything like it before. For fire burns while it has fuel: wood, gas, or some other material. But when the fuel has been consumed, the fire goes out. The fuel is finite, and once it is gone, the fire no longer burns.

We humans are like fire in that we have a finite amount of substance to fuel our lives. We have limited time to live; our understanding is limited by history and circumstance; our capacity to love is limited by our affections, and often fails when we come into conflict with others. Our life powers are limited, much to our chagrin.

Moses was a man who was intensely aware of his limitation: he couldn't speak properly; he had run away from his people whom he knew to be suffering; he had even killed a person. He felt his shortcomings keenly. When God spoke to him from the burning bush and told him that he would send him to Pharoah to liberate the Israelites, Moses—feeling his limits and doubting his ability—replied: "Who am I, that I should go unto Pharaoh, and that I should bring forth the children of Israel out of Egypt?" (Exod 3:11)

---

1. Exod 3:2 (King James Version: all subsequent citations are from this version).

Because Moses felt and knew his limitation, he was prepared to become a spokesperson for God (a prophet); his sensing the truth of himself readied him to respond to God. We, too, may heed the promptings of truth about ourselves, and be led by the seed of God within. We, too, may be given to see the Light, to know Eternal Life that is beyond our finitude; we, too, may be delivered from captivity and led into the promised land.

Contrarily, we may be hemmed in, enslaved by the inward Pharoah. Who is this Pharoah within, who will not let us go? He it is who would prevail; who would control and dominate; and who'd refuse to see what is, in truth, immediately before him.

To Moses, who saw his limitation and confessed his need for strength, God replied: "Certainly I will be with thee" (Exod 3:12). The power and wisdom of God, Christ the Light Within, visits, empowers, and sustains our lives indefinitely, eternally. Like a fire whose fuel is not consumed in burning is the life he brings to us: a life whose substance is not consumed in time but is eternal.

The New Way

[The following is based upon ministry given in a Philadelphia meeting on November 5, 2017.]

THERE IS A STORY about Jesus that takes place after he'd been ministering for a while. He was at home, visiting with his brothers shortly before a festival was to occur in Jerusalem. His brothers were planning to go to the festival, but Jesus was not planning to go with them. The brothers spoke to Jesus, perhaps to chastise him for not going or perhaps to mock him. They said to Jesus, if you have a message for the people, why don't you go to the festival and give it? No one who wants to be known acts in secret. Show yourself to the world. Jesus responds by saying: "My time is not yet come: but your time is alway ready."[1]

What Jesus is saying here is that he must wait for guidance before he acts; he doesn't act on his own power and volition, as do his brothers, but he waits until he's been given understanding from God for what he is to do, and when he is to do it. It is a new way to be, to regulate one's life. And this is the content of Jesus's ministry: there's something new.

When I come to meeting, I arrive early and, a little while later, listen as people begin to enter the meeting room and settle in. I like to hear all the sounds: the coughing, the sniffling, the shuffling of feet. These are cozy human sounds; there's a warmth in hearing them, like sitting in front of a fire. And then there are the messages: people's opinions and ideas. People have always had opinions and ideas. They, too, are human, a natural part of us. Some may be good ideas and some not; some may be productive and others destructive; some dutiful and others careless; some creative and others unimaginative, but whatever their qualities, they are all ideas. They

---

1. John 7:6 (King James Version).

come with our being human, along with all the other capacities that have been given to us by our Creator.

When Jesus spoke about his time being "not yet come," but his brothers' time being "alway[s] ready," he was making a distinction between the new nature and power he'd been given by God—an inspired, divine nature—and the old human nature in which we are confined to knowing and receiving only human ideas and opinions.

To inform, to manifest, and to witness to this new way of being—partaking of the divine nature—was the purpose of Jesus's ministry; it is the new way given by God.

Sifting the Heart
Some Observations on the Second Chapter of Matthew

To believe that wherever the true Gospel is proclaimed with power, men will open their hearts without further difficulty, is a mistaken optimism. Rather, a living proclamation of the Gospel often sifts the hearts of men, and the more powerful the message the more violent is the hostility of the powers of darkness. Hence it is precisely those Christians who have the deepest Christian experience, who have the greatest personal experience of the reality of the power of Darkness. —*Emil Brunner*

BRUNNER'S ASSERTION THAT "a living proclamation of the Gospel often sifts the hearts of men" is illustrated in the second chapter of Matthew. Here is a story that focuses on the contrasting responses to Jesus's birth: the response of Herod the king is contrasted to that of the wise men from the east. This topic of differing reactions to the appearance of Christ occurs very early in Matthew's gospel, immediately after the genealogy and description of the circumstances of the birth. That these opposite reactions hold a prime position at the beginning of this book suggests their matter is of foremost relevance when considering Jesus's purpose in coming into the world: his appearing acts as a catalyst that precipitates reaction or movement in man at the most profound level, the level at which his life is orchestrated and determined.

As did the characters in this story, each of us must answer the question posed by Christ's coming into the world: Is this new being worthy of worship, or is he to be rejected and destroyed? Confronted with this dilemma, each from his inmost heart will declare his fealty: whether to God or to Satan; whether to Truth or to deceit; whether to good or to evil; to life or to death; to Being or to nothingness. The power of God has come into our midst, and we can no longer entertain a clouded, indeterminate awareness; Christ the light reveals what darkness has hidden.

Verses 1 and 2 introduce the main characters—Herod and the wise men—and the contrasts between them are immediately evident. Herod is king of Judaea where the birth occurs, and the wise men have come from the distant east. Coming from another land, they have news that Herod, who sits as king in control of his provincial domain, does not have; for knowledge of Christ does not arise from the narrow, localized self; it comes from another place. Interpreted, knowledge of Christ does not arise from earthly man; it is given from heaven, which is far from the earthly, and "a better country" (Heb 11:16)."[1]

Whereas the wise men, recognize the new-born king as worthy of their journeying and their worship, Herod (and all his domain with him) are troubled by the news of the birth of the "King of the Jews" (Matt 2:3). In fear of being displaced by the new king, Herod marshals his resources, calling together his priests and scribes, who correctly identify Bethlehem as the birthplace of the Messiah.[2]

Herod relies on a different source for his information than do the wise men: he turns to prophetic writings to learn where the birth is to take place (Mic 5:2). By contrast, the wise men rely on the heavenly portent—the star—to locate the place of birth. That is to say, the earthly one looks to the written record of the past, while the wise ones look to the light of heaven. The earthly have a preserved, static record to inform them, while the wise turn to the active and present light for guidance.

Though Herod can place the location of the birth, he cannot know the time, for time is a medium of change, and Herod only has access to the

---

1. *Epigraph.* Brunner, *Creation*, 145. Heb 11:16 (King James Version; all subsequent citations are from this version).

2. As to the birthplace, the two sources (prophetic writings [5] and the star [9]) agree: both indicate Bethlehem. Thus--the narrator is telling us--the Jewish Scriptures confirm Jesus as the Messiah. Of the four canonical gospels, the book of Matthew is considered to be the most Jewish, emphasizing the validity of the Law and the prophets and asserting Christ Jesus's rightful position within the tradition. In addition to the prophecy naming Bethlehem as the birthplace of the Messiah (the ruler of the people Israel [6]), this chapter contains three additional references to Old Testament prophecies and their fulfillment in Jesus: these are found in verses 15, 18, and 23. Written between 70 and 80 AD, the book of Matthew exemplifies a Jewish-Christian perspective.

inert words of history. Therefore, he asks the wise ones, "what time the star appeared" (2:7). This cooperative exchange of information of the birth's location and time suggests the two parties share a common intent, and Herod exploits that false assumption by requesting the wise ones reveal the child's whereabouts once he's been found, "that I may come and worship him also" (2:8). Herod's intent is not to worship (2:6) but to destroy (2:16), and with this act of deceit, Herod declares his fealty to death and the devil. In pursuing the death of the Christ through ordaining the death of the innocents (2:16), it is inevitable and just that it is Herod himself who dies in this story (2:19). So dies the soul of any who act in deceit.

The wise ones, having departed from Herod, follow the light of heaven to the new birth. We are told, the star "stood over where the young child was" (2:9), which is to say the light is a reliable guide that leads its followers to a place where it rests over and upon the new birth. It is a place of rest, discovered within, where we, too, may "rejoice[d] with exceeding great joy" (2:10). As Herod's act of deceit declared his dark conspiracy with evil, the wise ones' actions, in contrast, demonstrate their fealty to the new King. They have traveled to a new place; they have sought and found; they have rejoiced, worshiped, and offered their gifts. Unlike Herod, they continue to live throughout the remainder of the story, having wisely "departed into their own country another way" (2:12), a way unknown to the Herods of the world.

In departing to "their own country" (their true home), the wise are given heavenly direction, this time coming from a dream. As there were four Old Testament prophecies fulfilled in this story, there are likewise four dreams that offer direction, again showing a continuity and balance between old and the new: between what has been given by God formerly and what is presently given now. Each dream directs a change of location: the wise men are to return to their country by a different way; Joseph is to take his family to Egypt; and once Herod is dead, he's directed by the same angel to bring them back to Israel (20). Once in Israel, Joseph dreams of God's warning and turns aside to settle in Nazareth. Thus the story ends with a fulfilled prophecy (Judg 13:5): "He shall be called a Nazarene" (Matt 2:23).

This early chapter in Matthew sets the stage for more particular explorations of the themes it's introduced. Foremost is the message that the arrival of Christ upon earth will sift the heart of each person, resulting in either one's salvation or one's condemnation. Respectively, the heart will know life and joy, or it will remain captivated by fear, rage, and death: one or the other will result; there are no exemptions nor obfuscations to be had. Secondly, that although past prophecy has validity, its efficacy and influence is now superseded by the present, active light of heaven, which is Christ. Finally, this chapter's end note and destination tells us the true Light/Word is now become flesh, and is, in fact, "a Nazarene" (2:23). Previewed in this chapter are the consequences that result from the momentous event of the new birth, the coming of the Lord. We are prepared to read on.

Righteousness Fulfilled
Some Observations on the Third Chapter of Matthew

[R]eligion is a pure stream of righteousness flowing from the image of God, and is the life and power of God planted in the heart and mind by the law of life, which bringeth the soul, mind, spirit, and body to be conformable to God, the Father of spirits, and to Christ; so that they come to have fellowship with the Father and the son, and with all his holy angels and saints.—*George Fox*

UPON ENTERING THE CATHEDRAL of Pisa on a visit to that city twenty years ago and walking a short distance along the nave toward the altar, I came across two small bronze sculptures, directly across from one another on either side of the center aisle. As I recall, each free-standing sculpted figure was about two feet high and placed on a small pedestal that brought the piece to eye level. On the right stood John the Baptist and, on the left, Jesus. As the two works had been made by the same artist in the same material and style and placed directly across the nave one from the other, they stood in mirror-like relationship. Thus, the art conveyed the theological idea that Jesus and John the Baptist are alike, and yet different.

In the third chapter of Matthew, the characters of John the Baptist and Jesus together work to convey an idea: the righteous stance of man is prelude to the divine nature of Christ. Where we are in our first-birth, earthly nature can—and must—be moved into the second-birth, the heavenly nature. In its layout, chapter 3 is structured to illustrate this idea: the beginning verses are given to John, the prophet born of woman,[1] and the ending verses to Jesus, the "beloved Son," born of God (Matt 3:17).

In the first few verses of this chapter, we learn about the Baptist: how he lives and what he does. John stations himself in the wilderness, and what he wears and eats is of little concern to him (Matt 3:4). In the silence of solitude, away from society's pursuits and distractions, he attends to the inward claim upon him, rather than the outward clamor around him. John's work is to prepare the way of the Lord (3:3), and so he preaches: "Repent ye: for the kingdom of heaven is at hand" (3:2). His call to repentance is not some meager scolding to elicit remorse or sadness for a misstep but a challenge to recalibrate the inward vantage point of one's being.

The focus of the narrative widens to include John's placement in and effect upon society. Verse 3 has settled him securely within the history of Israel: he is the prophet foretold by the prophet Isaiah, who envisioned John's ministry to the society of his day.[2] Both city and country folk flock to him in his solitary abode: responding to his call, confessing their sins, and seeking the change his baptism signifies. John draws people to righteousness and holiness . . . but not all people.

In chapter 2, the wise men from the east came to worship the new king, while Herod attempted to slay him. In chapter 3, clear lines are again drawn between those who respond favorably to the appearance of the righteous, and those who do not. In verses 5 through 10, a distinction is made between the receptive folk of "all Judea" (3:5) and the venomous Pharisees and the Sadducees (3:7). By the time this group arrives at the Jordan, they have been sized up by John and given no opportunity to speak, no chance to strike (3:7). Their "religion" has come from their association with others: "We have Abraham to our father" (3:9), they say within themselves. Relying on the pedigree of one's social or historical connection, however, is not the substance of true religion. Rather, as stated by Fox, "religion is a pure stream of righteousness flowing from the image of God." Each of these two diametric dispositions produces its own commensurate fruit, and John informs the hypocrites, they will be like trees "hewn down, and cast into the fire" (3:10).

---

1. *Epigraph*. Fox, *Works*, 1:411. Matt 11:11 (King James Version; all subsequent citations are from this version).

2. As in the previous chapter, the narrator asserts Jewish tradition confirms the new.

Righteousness Fulfilled

The first twelve verses of the chapter have prefaced the primary theme: divine nature comes to those who accept the responsibility of knowing themselves to be created in the image of the righteous God.

As we near the end of the narrative, we see the two main figures—John and Jesus—for a moment inhabiting a kind of stasis or a state of equilibrium where John ("none greater born of women" [Matt 11:11]), having ascended to his highest potential, hovers, as Jesus, the heavenly man, readies himself to receive Sonship. It is a touching moment of beauty, where the nobility of the human spirit is seen and quietly appreciated. A sweet exchange ensues between the two over who will baptize whom. Each defers to the other, not as polite nicety but that their course of action may be rightly ordered. For both men recognize righteousness to be their rule: the single and only pathway that leads from earth to heaven, from the earthly nature into the divine. "For thus it becometh us to fulfil all righteousness" (3:15), Jesus reasons with John, and John, in righteousness, obeys the one who is "mightier than [he]" (3:11).

The final verses of this third chapter of Matthew display the culminating moment to which all that has passed before has led: here is man transformed into his divine nature. John the Baptist had risen to the peak of human capacity, and from that point, Jesus, now baptized, continues upward in straight, righteous ascent: he "went up straightway out of the water" to find "the heavens were opened unto him (3:16)." That is to say, in Jesus Christ, God reveals himself to man. In love to humanity, the Spirit of God descends and lights upon us (3:16), and in this revelation, we are given to know the divine nature present within. Through receiving the Spirit/Word of God, the rightness of being is known unequivocally and in fullness and confirmed extant forever. "This is my beloved Son, in whom I am well pleased (17:5).

The Mind of Christ

For it hath been declared unto me of you . . . that there are contentions among you. Now this I say, that every one of you saith, I am of Paul; and I of Apollos; and I of Cephas; and I of Christ. Is Christ divided? Was Paul crucified for you? Or were ye baptized in the name of Paul? . . . For Christ sent me not to baptize, but to preach the gospel: not with wisdom of words, lest the cross of Christ should be made of none effect. For the preaching of the cross is to them that perish foolishness; but unto us which are saved it is the power of God (1 Cor 1:11–13, 17–18).

> What I mean is this: each of you is saying, "I am Paul's man", or "I am for Apollos"; "I follow Cephas", or "I am Christ's." . . . Christ did not send me to baptize, but to proclaim the Gospel; and to do it without relying on the language of worldly wisdom, so that the fact of Christ on his cross might have its full weight. This doctrine of the cross is sheer folly to those on their way to ruin, but to us who are on the way to salvation it is the power of God (1 Cor 1:12, 17–18).[1]

> For Christ did not send me forth to baptize, but to preach the gospel; not in accomplished oratory, but so that the cross of the Christ might not be made meaningless. For the word of the cross is folly to those who go the way of perdition, but to us who go the way of salvation it is the power of God (1 Cor 1:17–18).[2]

IN THIS PASSAGE FROM the first epistle to the Corinthians,[3] Paul dismisses as trivial the quarrel that has divided the church: members have allied

---

1. *Epigraph.* 1 Cor 1:11–13, 17–18 (King James Version). 1 Cor 1:12, 17–18 (The New English Bible).
2. 1 Cor 1:17–18 (The New Testament translated by Richmond Lattimore).
3. I've used three Bible versions in this essay: the King James Version (KJV), The New

themselves with—and perhaps sought baptism from—one of several visiting apostles, and thereby have put themselves at odds with one another. Whichever visiting speaker has most impressed with "wisdom of words" has gained a particular following within the group. Paul will have none of it; chastises their divisiveness; and redirects their attention to the one essential, unifying power: the cross of Christ.

Having sensed the root of the problem to be a misbegotten debate of ideas, Paul then devotes the remainder of this first chapter, as well as the entirety of second, to illustrating the difference between thought and revelation, contrasting their respective origins, natures, and effects.

Ideas and opinions come about through the use of the intellect, and as intelligence has been the primary means by which these Corinthians—as well as the rest of humanity—have survived and thrived, Paul must express and convince them of the reality of the superior power that is hidden from but nonetheless calls to them. His first move is to debunk their "faith" in their intelligence to discern and know the things of God, and so he draws from the authority of Scripture[4] to show the dictum on the matter: "I will destroy the wisdom of the wise, and will bring to nothing the understanding of the prudent" (1 Cor 1:19 [KJV]). To drive home the point that intellect is not to be revered above its place (which is to say, intellect is not to be idolized), Paul assumes a tone of mockery and fires a smattering of rhetorical questions in the Greeks' direction: "Where is the sage? Where is the scholar? Where is the student of the age? Did not God turn the wisdom of the world to folly?" (1:20 [RL]) The world's wisdom is chided as futile: incapable of coming into the knowledge of God.

Reversals of worldly expectation abound throughout the remainder of this first chapter, for example: "the folly of God is wiser than men, and the weakness of God is stronger than men" (1:25 [RL]). All serve to deflate the intellect's suppositions and over-estimation of its reach and compass, necessary if one is to learn that "there is no place for human pride in the presence of God" (1:29 [NEB]). Yet having upended the doings of the Corinthians, Paul takes care to redirect their hope and confidence toward their proper destination: "You are in Christ Jesus by God's act, for God has made

---

English Bible (NEB), and The New Testament translated by Richmond Lattimore (RL). My choice of which version to use at any given point in the essay depended upon which of the three best provided clarity and meaning through the wording of the verse in question. Following each quotation, I identify which of the three versions I've used.

4. "[F]or the wisdom of their wise men shall perish, and the understanding of their prudent men shall be hid" (Isa 29:14b [KJV]).

him our wisdom; he is our righteousness; in him we are consecrated and set free" (1:30 [NEB]).

In chapter 2, Paul describes in more detail the differences between the power of God and the wisdom of men: he asserts the former can supply words whose import is hidden from even the most privileged, astute natural man, and available only to those initiated into the knowledge of God. Again, turning to Isaiah for authority,[5] Paul puts the wisdom of God out of reach of men's way of knowing—through eyes, ears, or heart—until God reveals by his Spirit "the things which God hath prepared for them that love him" (1 Cor 2:9 [KJV]). Repeatedly throughout this chapter, Paul emphasizes the fact that discernment and judgment are available to the person who knows God but remain inaccessible to even the most intellectually diligent and capable (6–8, 9–10, 11–13, and 14–15).

It is at the start of chapter 2, however, that Paul identifies the fulcrum on which the great transition or movement from natural to spiritual rests. He writes: "And I, brethren, when I came to you, came not with excellency of speech or of wisdom, declaring unto you the testimony of God. For I determined not to know any thing among you, save Jesus Christ, and him crucified (2:1–2 [KJV]).

What does Paul mean by his bald statement that his intention was to know only Jesus Christ crucified? How does this phrase express the distinction made between intellect—our natural power of discernment—and the transcendent wisdom that must be bestowed from above? What was it Christ knew and expressed on the cross that Paul asserts is the one essential thing to be known? It comes to this: By God's Will alone are we sustained in the glory of Life; this is a verity that must be birthed in the heart, not adopted by the mind.

Having accepted God's Will for himself, Jesus, the Christ on the cross, had ousted every impulse toward (and was deprived of) the comforts and powers that worldly life can supply. Nevertheless, in faith he was sustained and lifted up into Life by the power of God. We likewise may be lifted up into the glory of the Light of Christ, while concomitantly discovering that even our most virtuous thoughts and intents (though seeming to affirm, comfort, and enable us) do but intrude upon and dim the pure joy in the Light of his Presence. It is in that Light of Christ that the distinction

---

5. "For since the beginning of the world men have not heard, nor perceived by the ear, neither hath the eye seen, O God, beside thee, what he hath prepared for him that waiteth for him" (Isa 64:4 [KJV]).

The Mind of Christ

between Spirit and intellect is clearly felt and known, as surely as the difference between life and death.

In the beginning pages of his journal, George Fox compares the superior beneficence of the Lord to the best the world has to offer:

> I found two thirsts in me; the one after the creatures, to have got help and strength there; and the other after the Lord the creator, and his son Jesus Christ; and I saw all the world could do me no good. If I had had a king's diet, palace, and attendance, all would have been as nothing; for nothing gave me comfort but the Lord by his power.[6]

We, too, can be preoccupied with the pains or pleasures of worldly life, including intellectual activity, but can learn to set them all aside in order to wait open and empty to receive Christ. He appears and presents himself as pure Light, perfectly and fully overriding whatever our particular worldly condition had been in the moment previous. Any imposition of thought, however virtuous—such as questioning how to be of help to others in spiritual matters—pollutes (a strong but accurate word) the purity of the Presence. Use and service to others must be found in refraining from impinging upon the purity of the Light within. In its purity is its power, and any imposition made upon it interferes with that purity and thus its power. When present and turned to, the Light does overcome any dark thoughts which detract from being, whether virtuous or vicious. To be conscious of the purity of the Light is to sense its saving, sanctifying power. From this personal reflection, one may infer that it is through the power of the Light of Christ that the world comes to be redeemed, which is, of course, a message confirmed by our tradition.

> So the Lord God almighty preserve you in that which is pure, up to himself, who is pure, to receive his wisdom, and that with it and in it, ye all may come to be ordered to his glory, who is God over all; to whom be all honour and glory, God blessed for ever; that with it ye may come to see the lamb of God, the saviour of your souls, who was, before the letter was.[7]

Paul ends this second chapter by stating one last capacity that distinguishes the natural (sensual) man from the one who is gifted with the Spirit: the power to judge justly. He then concludes his lesson with the simple,

---

6. Fox, *Works*, 1:75.
7. Fox, *Works*, 7:48–49.

triumphant claim of the Spirit of Christ incarnate. "But he that is spiritual judgeth all things, yet he himself is judged of no man. For who hath known the mind of the Lord, that he may instruct him? But we have the mind of Christ" (2:15–16 [KJV]).

Introduction to Lewis Benson Lectures

In 1976 at Haverford College near Philadelphia, Pennsylvania, Lewis Benson delivered a series of five lectures titled *A New Foundation to Build On*. The following two essays introduce two of those lectures: "The Power of the Gospel" and "The Gospel and Self-Knowledge." Following these two are an additional seven essays introducing Benson's lectures from another series titled *Rediscovering the Teaching of George Fox*. This second series was given at Moorestown (N.J.) Meeting in 1982.[1]

INTRODUCTION TO "THE POWER OF THE GOSPEL"

The Quakers revolution was a movement to recover the experience of the power of God through the recovery of that gospel of power which had been lost "since the Apostles' days."—Lewis Benson

In August 1976 at Haverford College, near Philadelphia, Pennsylvania, Lewis Benson gave a series of five lectures tiled "A New Foundation to Build On." The second lecture in this series is called "The Power of the Gospel." It begins with a brief history of George Fox's early years at the time he felt near despair of finding a way to live a right and true life, a crisis that was resolved when he was given to know Christ experientially. In this lecture, Benson alludes to the same stultifying difficulty early in his own life. As a result of having passed from darkness to light, both Fox and Benson, for the remainder of their lives, made their first concern the presentation of the gospel and its message, for the gospel conveyed the power to overcome the human condition of alienation from God.

---

1. All lectures in these two series (including those not introduced in the text) can be found on the New Foundation Fellowship website, nffquaker.org, under the Resources tab. *Epigraph*. Benson, "Power of Gospel," 2.

Though Scriptures bear witness to the availability of and necessity for coming into the gospel, the church of Fox's time no longer taught this message, and it was no longer known. Isolated groups throughout the centuries had known and practiced this faith, but it had been absent from the church for 1600 years. It was the Quaker mission to recover the gospel and present it to the world.

Benson spends a major portion of the lecture describing the content of the gospel message that Quakers preached; it was most briefly formulated in the statement "Christ is come to teach his people himself." In the seventeenth century, this summary expressed a unique understanding of Christ's salvific work: his being present and active, with particular emphasis on his prophetic office or function as the teacher of righteousness.

> Whenever [Fox] preached the gospel, he preached the "offices of Christ," and especially the office of prophet, because it is by hearing Christ the prophet that the knowledge of God's righteousness is received and the power to obey is given.[2]

The lecture concludes by referring to the 1945 discovery of the Dead Sea Scrolls, a discovery that confirmed seventeenth-century Friends' assertion that the gospel they preached was the same that was held by the Jewish Christians of the first century. Though it was a significant discovery, it had little impact on Quakers then or since, nor on Christians in general, for an apostasy is overcome not through gospel-corroborating scholarship but through the gospel itself.

INTRODUCTION TO "THE GOSPEL AND SELF-KNOWLEDGE"

"THE GOSPEL AND SELF-KNOWLEDGE" is the fourth of five lectures in the series titled *A New Foundation to Build On*, given by Lewis Benson in 1976 in Haverford, Pennsylvania. Benson begins this fourth lecture with a survey of types of religious consciousness that characterized different historical periods. His review provides context for the primary focus of the lecture: our modern era, which began more than a century ago. Benson contends modern "mass man" no longer sustains an integrated identity; this calamity

---

2. Benson, "Power of Gospel," 3.

Introduction to Lewis Benson Lectures

manifests itself widely in the personal sense of "lostness." This feeling of being lost and the subsequent search for identity is, Benson asserts, the distinguishing ethos of our age.

Wide-ranging, broad analysis is uncommon among scholars, and the reader's immediate reaction may be to discount grand-scale assertions as devoid of nuance, and therefore inaccurate. Such a prejudice might arise in those who've yet to come to a vantage point from which can be seen the essential properties of different religious understandings. This vista is one Benson can and does offer in this lecture, and here he states his theme:

> The purpose of this paper is to compare some modern philosophical approaches to the problem of self-knowledge to the prophetic Christian understanding as exemplified by George Fox.[3]

The first philosophy Benson brings to light is the system of self-realization that was set forth by George Gurdjieff,[4] an early-twentieth-century teacher with whom Benson studied as a young man. Though Benson did not find in Gurdjieff that which he sought, he was, nevertheless, strongly affected by his time spent in Gurdjieff's compound near Paris. This impact is evidenced in the disproportionate attention given in the lecture to Gurdjieff's understanding of the problem of self, and his method of developing consciousness through motivated self-interest and disciplined control of the will. Benson later came to realize that Gurdjieff's reliance on methodology signaled its faulty grounding in human endeavor, and thus revealed its disparity with the prophetic faith of George Fox that Benson later came to know and affirm.

Benson next moves through a brief summary of both the techniques and suppositions found in Socrates's philosophy and in classic Western Mysticism—giving each but a paragraph to set out their respective deficiencies. He then proceeds to his main topic, the Christian approach to the problem of self-knowledge.

> The Christian approach to the problem of self-knowledge takes as its starting point the view of man that is set forth in the Bible: that people were not created to have a self-conscious existence

---

3. Benson, "Self-Knowledge," 1.

4. George Gurdjieff was a Russian spiritual teacher of Armenian and Greek descent. He was born in the mid-nineteenth century and died in 1949. Gurdjieff taught that consciousness is fragmented in most human beings, and discipline is needed to integrate mind, emotion, and body. He developed and taught a method for reaching full potential of consciousness, which entailed Movements and exercises involving sensation.

independent of God. It is the Creator who reveals what is good and what is evil. Man's life is characterized by his dependence on God. When this relationship is broken, the primary law of man's being is broken, and his life becomes a deformation of the life intended for him by the Creator.[5]

Benson turns to Emil Brunner, a prominent Protestant (Reformed) theologian of the last century, who affirms Benson's position: man's self-realization is contingent upon his response to God's call. From there, Benson brings George Fox into the discussion, as one whose initial, broken condition became apparent through receiving Christ, the Light, revealing the self: "With the light man sees himself, which light comes from Christ." [6]

Additionally, by obedience to the inward teaching of the Light, man is restored to right relationship with God. The Light of Christ is the revealer and teacher of a new righteousness, which judges out not only deeds that are manifestly evil but also those deeds which arise from the attempt to live a moral life outside of God and Christ: these attempts, too, are brought under condemnation by the Light. Fox says: "The light lets you see your deeds . . . whether they be wrought in God or no."[7]

The deeds "wrought in God" is the righteousness that God calls for, as distinguished from humanly discerned self-righteousness, which is often—through ignorance or pride—wrongly attributed to God. Such deeds arise from the less-than-human self "that is gradually formed in us as we attempt to find ourselves outside of God and God's word to us."[8] That self, says Fox, has the "nature of brute beasts,"[9] and must be denied. Neither the self-knowledge nor self-righteousness that is assumed independent of the Light can begin to approximate the perfection that accompanies our restoration to the image of God in Christ.

In contrast to Gurdjieff's, others' philosophy, or theories of psychology that claim self-realization is a function of man's will and power to uncover his essential being, Fox holds that human personality, or self, is universally fallen and deformed into a sub-human condition, and that we can be restored to our true, intended state only when recast through "hearing and

---

5. Benson, "Self-Knowledge," 3.
6. Fox, *Works*, 7:142, as quoted in Benson, "Self-Knowledge," 4.
7. Fox, *Works*, 1:83, as quoted in Benson, "Self-Knowledge," 4.
8. Benson, "Self-Knowledge," 4.
9. Fox, *Works*, 4:35.

obeying the speaking God."[10] "The self or false personality is "judged out" by the light and a new life appears in them who "walk in him the new and living way, out of the old way."[11]

The sense of "lostness" that modern man inevitably endures indicates inner change is needed: the revealing of and standing against evil within has not yet taken place; the self or false personality has not yet been denied; the second birth not yet been undergone. Fox's prescription for this lost, fallen condition is this:

> [W]ait upon God in that which is pure . . . and stand still in . . . to see your savior to make you free from that which the light doth discover to you to be evil.[12]

In Christ there is freedom from sin, and only there does one find unity and "fellowship with all who believe in the light, hear the light, obey the light and walk in the light."[13]

INTRODUCTION TO "THE PLACE OF GEORGE FOX IN CHRISTIAN HISTORY"

In this lecture, Benson states his intention for the series: "to focus on Fox's actual teachings as revealed in his writings," thereby addressing two problems: (1) scholars' mistaken interpretations of Fox's teaching, and (2) widespread lack of familiarity with our Quaker heritage. These lectures provide an excellent opportunity for Friends to familiarize themselves with significant portions of early Quaker understanding, as Benson's scholarship is thorough; his interpretation is sound; and his presentations are clear and coherent.

I always try to approach people's interpretations of Fox with an open mind, but I've often found that he's misrepresented and misunderstood. Lewis Benson also saw this problem and identified it in this lecture, referring to many scholars of his time.

One of the primary distinctions that Fox makes is that there is a pure religion "that comes down from above" (Benson identifies this elsewhere

---

10. Benson, "Self-Knowledge," 4.
11. Fox, *Works*, 8:52, as quoted in Benson, "Self-Knowledge," 5.
12. Fox, *Works*, 7:24, as quoted in Benson, "Self-Knowledge," 5.
13. Benson, "Self-Knowledge," 5.

as "Abrahamic religion"), and then there is manmade religion ("Adamic religion"), which is arrived at by means of ideas, emotions, ideals, social pressures, etc., in short, anything human beings can contrive and subscribe to. In this all-too-prevalent manmade religion (Adamic religion), Person A will likely have a different take on religion from Person B. If, however, they each are choosing and forming their religion from ideas, feelings, principles, etc., they both are subscribing to manmade religion. An example of this apparently-different-but-actually-the-same manmade religion is Protestants and Catholics: though differing, were nevertheless of the same root and stock, claimed the seventeenth-century Quakers.

In contrast to the Adamic religion that permeated their culture, what Fox and first Friends were given was the pure religion that comes down from above, i.e., revelation. (Recall Fox's surprise at hearing "There is one, Christ Jesus, that can speak to thy condition.") Now this Word is what is revealed by Christ, and is Christ, and is unchanging; it is the gospel, the power of God. Therefore, those who have received this gospel power find themselves in unity with those in history (first Friends, apostles) who had also received this heavenly dispensation. Because of that unity of spirit, we find that the words of these two groups convey our own most inward identity and also present wisdom that we can affirm, ascribe to, and benefit from.

The faith that comes down from above cannot be acquired by human beings; it must be given by God. So, what does one do? Letting John the Baptist's words resonate within one's heart might be useful, as he came before the Lord and prepared the way. Ultimately, it's about needing truth for your soul like you need oxygen for your body. I see this particular sense of the need for truth to be the hallmark of humanity, but people deny their humanity often. The words from the Gospel of John speak to this denial: "He came unto his own, and his own received him not."[14]

Meanwhile, we have a great deal of literature that affirms the reality of the gospel power. I've heard a number of people say they were convinced of the gospel by reading Fox. I've always found this suspect because one is assimilating ideas when one reads, and Life is not intellect, and neither is it emotion. Fox does affirm—throughout all his voluminous writings—the reality of the new, inward Life that God in His mercy and truth meets out to those who call upon Him in their need, to those who wait in readiness. There are quite a few of Jesus's parables about preparing oneself. Most

---

14. John 1:11 (King James Version; all subsequent citations are from this version).

emphatic, however, is Jesus's concluding lesson to his disciples shortly before he's arrested:

> Watch ye therefore: for ye know not when the master of the house cometh, at even, or at midnight, or at the cockcrowing, or in the morning: Lest coming suddenly he find you sleeping. And what I say unto you I say unto all, Watch.[15]

INTRODUCTION TO "THE EVERLASTING GOSPEL PREACHED BY GEORGE FOX"

Ye that have seen the everlasting gospel, and known the everlasting gospel preached again, which was among the apostles, and have been reaped out from among the apostates, got up since the apostles' days; I say, live in it, and dwell in it; in which life and power ye see over to the apostles' days.—George Fox

In this lecture, Benson identifies the heart of Fox's message: Christ Jesus is alive and present among us in a functional way through the inward exercise of his offices. "Christ is come to teach his people himself" is the shorthand version of Fox's message. It was the recovery of this gospel message, which had been lost since apostolic times that enabled the early Quaker missionaries to preach the same message with the same power that had been known to the apostles.

With the recovery of the gospel, the power of God, Friends expected a new era in Christian history (one in which Christ is present, not absent), and this message drew many together into a people who received the living and present Christ as their prophet, priest, king, shepherd, and bishop. For as long as prophetic gospel ministers preached, the Quaker movement grew, for the gospel had power by which many who heard it were convinced and convicted. As the apostles were sent to teach and gather, so were the first Friends; both groups were commissioned and sent by the transcendent, living God. An excerpt from Edward Burrough's description of the Valiant 60's commission can be found in this lecture.[16]

---

15. Mark 13:35–37.
16. *Epigraph.* Fox, *Works,* 7:268.

INTRODUCTION TO "THE RELATION OF FOX'S MESSAGE TO THE BIBLE"

In Fox's teaching, however, the prophetic office of Christ becomes no less important than his priestly and kingly functions, and this shift of emphasis brings about a Copernican revolution in our understanding of who Jesus Christ is and how he saves people.[17] —Lewis Benson

Since apostolic times, many differing Christologies have been presented by institutions and reformers, and various gospels have been preached. George Fox, however, recovered the primitive Christian witness with its emphasis on the prophetic office of Christ. In the third of his lectures given at the Moorestown, New Jersey, meetinghouse in 1982, Lewis Benson credits Fox with rediscovering this ancient, apostolic testimony and then goes on to examine its basis in Old Testament promises; prophecies; and figures, types, and shadows.

Friends distinctive doctrines of perfection and continuing revelation trace their origin to Fox's recovery of the everlasting gospel of Christ as the prophet who speaks to us from heaven, which Benson affirms in the following statement from this lecture:

> When [Fox] preached that "Christ has come to teach his people himself," he was proclaiming that Christ is the expected "prophet like Moses" who is able to teach us what is right and what is wrong, and to give us the power to do the right and reject the wrong. He is able to save us from sin, and not, as the Calvinists maintain, unable to do more than save us from its consequences.[18]

INTRODUCTION TO "THE NEW WORSHIP"

Fox repeats this call over and over: "Keep your testimony . . . for your worship in the spirit and in the truth, that Christ Jesus hath set up"; "keep up your testimony in the light, power, and spirit of God, for the worship that Christ set up above sixteen hundred years since, in spirit and in truth . . . which is a worship that cannot be shaken."[19] This is a testimony that the Quakers had before the

---

17. *Epigraph.* Benson, "Fox's Message," 14.
18. Benson, "Fox's Message," 14–15.
19. *Epigraph.* Benson, "New Worship," 21. Fox, *Works*, 8:84, as quoted in Benson, 5.

peace testimony was formulated in 1660, and I think in Fox's mind it was the most important of the Quaker testimonies. It is the thing that brings people to Christ, as they see that we are gathering together to feel his living presence in our midst.—Lewis Benson

In the fourth lecture of the series, Benson examines the origin and nature of early Quaker worship. His intent is "to get a new perspective on the problems of contemporary Quakerism, and to bring something into the life of the Society of Friends today which is the heritage of all Quakers but has not survived in any living tradition."[20]

There is an assumption among Liberal Quakers that waiting in silence during the hour of worship replicates the early Quaker practice, an assumption which fails to take into account that the intent of early Quakers was entirely different from that of contemporaries, which centers on personal reflection that is sequentially shared. Early Quaker worship was attended by "people who had heard and received this everlasting gospel and who were filled with a fervent desire to gather together in the name of Jesus to wait to feel his presence in their midst as their living teacher, leader, ruler, counsellor, and orderer."[21] Early Friends gathered together and quieted themselves in order to receive and hear their heavenly prophet, receive intercession from their heavenly priest, be ruled as a people by their heavenly king, and be fed by their heavenly shepherd. Their cohesion was the result of waiting together for guidance, acceptance, and instruction that came from heaven, and not from one another's personal perspectives.

> For Fox, meeting in the name of Jesus has a very definite content, and it has to do with the gospel experience, the experience of Christ as present, and present in a functioning way. I have found 22 references where Fox makes it clear that "meeting in the name" involves such a definite experience.[22]

That this revolutionary way of worship should have been lost from Quaker communities over the last several hundred years is not surprising; for it had likewise been lost since the apostles' days and not recovered until the early Quakers practiced it 1600 years later. Yet corporate worship in spirit and in truth, meeting "in the name of Jesus," remains forever

---

20. Benson, "New Worship," 21.
21. Benson, "New Worship," 21.
22. Benson, "New Worship," 23.

available to reclaim yet once more by any who come to be "children of the New Covenant."

INTRODUCTION TO "THE NEW MINISTRY"

First, they must be made alive by Christ, [who] is alive and liveth forevermore . . . and quickened by him, before they . . . can be ministers of the spirit, [and] be able to receive heavenly and spiritual things. . . . So, all must be called by Christ . . . out of the world . . . and receive his power, spirit and grace and truth and faith [before] they can preach Christ. . . . They must see him and know him and hear his voice, and have spiritual things from him . . . and they must all receive their gifts from him for the work of their ministry. . . . It is Jesus Christ that doth make and ordain . . . ministers by his power and spirit.—George Fox

Having begun with some preliminary comments on the history of studies and efforts to rejuvenate vocal ministry since the mid-nineteenth century as well as references to present-day alternative interpretations of ministry work, Benson moves on to the lecture's main purpose: "to explore the implications for us today of the Everlasting Gospel that Fox preached, and especially to learn how it may bring us closer to the practice and experience of a living ministry."[23]

Fox believed that the preaching and receiving of the everlasting gospel would lead to the recovery of all that had been lost since the apostles' days. Benson states that it was recognized that "'many through his [Fox's] ministry were turned from darkness to light . . . for he did not preach himself but Jesus Christ.' Fox declared that 'the work of the ministry [is] to bring people to the knowledge of the son of God.'"[24]

Benson expands on the nature of gospel ministry work. He briefly covers the qualifications of a gospel minister (seen in the epigraph above) and speaks of the different approaches required for ministering to different groups of people. Ministering to the world ("breaking up the clods") is different from ministering to settled meetings ("keeping the sheep"). Whether threshing, plowing, or keeping the sheep, gospel ministers were intensely

---

23. *Epigraph.* Fox, Headley MSS, Cat. No. 8 102F, 320, as quoted in Benson, "New Ministry," 36. Benson, "New Ministry," 35.

24. Benson, "New Ministry," 35–36.

dedicated to their work. Meetings—both home and those visited—understood, valued, and supported prophetic, itinerant, non-professional ministers in their work, caring for their practical and personal needs.

One example of the latter is a recounting of an opportunity given Benson as a young minister, his receiving personal affirmation from a highly esteemed older minister. It was a memorable event for Benson that confirmed the weighty and wonderful calling he had been given.

Necessary to include in a talk on prophetic Quaker ministry is some discussion of its demise. Benson writes (in the early 1980s): "there are now very few who have knowledge from *experience* of the *itinerant, prophetic, non-professional* Quaker ministry. People have just never met a minister of the type that was characteristic of the Quaker ministry in the eighteenth or nineteenth centuries. . . . We know about it only by hearsay."[25] (Italics are Benson's.)

Benson ends this talk with an affirmation of gospel ministry's power to enliven and restore the true beginning and purpose of the original Quaker movement, as well as that of the apostles, which is to turn people from darkness to light through preaching the Word of God. The talk concludes:

> Now that the everlasting gospel is being preached once more, this will certainly lead to a better understanding of the ministry that belongs to this gospel and to the new covenant. The preaching of this gospel has begun to stimulate interest in the nature of Quaker ministry, and this is sure to be the case wherever the everlasting gospel is preached and received.[26]

INTRODUCTION TO "RESTORING THE CHURCH OF THE CROSS"

No longer do you keep in fellowship, but as you keep in the cross of Christ. . . . This fellowship is not of man, nor by man; for it is in the everlasting power of God.—George Fox

In this lecture, Benson explores the meaning and relevance of these theological terms: the cross of Christ; the church, as fellowship of the cross; the

---

25. Benson, "New Ministry," 35.
26. Benson, "New Ministry," 39.

righteousness that is given through Christ and defines the community; and the consequent suffering entailed in bearing witness to the Truth in a world devoid of understanding.

People gather and come together for many different reasons, but the church, as George Fox averred, was a coming together and fellowship of people who knew—understood through experience—the cross of Christ, and kept to it. Since the days of the apostles, the knowledge of the cross as the defining characteristic of the faith community had been lost, said Fox. This loss was called "the apostasy."

> Here began the apostasy . . . when they . . . apostatized from the true cross, the power of God, and from the true church.[27]

It was Fox's mission to bring people out of the apostasy, to gather a people to Christ by the power of the gospel. Benson writes:

> [Fox's] gospel message that "Christ has come to teach his people himself" is a call to people to become disciples of Christ, to be taught the principles of God's righteousness by him, and to come into a fellowship that learns together, obeys together, and suffers together.[28]

First Friends had discovered the one thing needful: the living purveyor of righteousness. Without the coming of Christ to teach his people his righteousness, no valid claim to righteousness could be—or can be—made: neither the Old Testament law in the apostles' days; nor the Bible's prescriptions in the seventeenth century; nor the testimonies and self-edification of our own times. Christ, the Lord of righteousness, "is not of man nor by man." Nor is the fellowship of Christ determined by man's rubrics.

> He that is in Christ, is at the end of the law, and the precepts, and the statutes, and the ordinances, and the commandments, and is in the substance, God's righteousness.[29]

Suffering for bearing witness to the Truth that comes from God and Christ is a well-known part of Quaker history, and Benson spends much of the latter part of this lecture discussing what precipitates suffering and how suffering for righteousness of Christ is distinct from other kinds of suffering. He writes:

27. *Epigraph.* Fox, *Works,* 8:67. Fox, *Works,* 4:171.
28. Benson, "Church of the Cross," 47.
29. Fox, *Works,* 3:270.

> Thus Fox is teaching that suffering, in the Christian sense, is for the sake of bearing a faithful testimony to the Truth that comes from God and Christ, and especially for the righteousness that comes from God and Christ.[30]

Ample supporting quotations in this and other lectures of this series may mislead readers into thinking that Benson's work is primarily a scholarly endeavor. Although he does present modern Friends with information and analysis of our Society's beginning, his intent is not confined to presenting his scholarship. Benson had undergone the inward dying to self that results from a keen drive to have something solid on which to stand as one assumes inward maturity, as well as gazes out and navigates life with all its pitfalls. Benson, as many others, had discovered the life that Fox, too, had discovered. For both men, the purpose and direction of the remainder of their lives was set: to communicate and to challenge lost and fearful humanity, floundering in apostasy, to once again come to the great discovery: Christ in whom there is "no shadow, variableness, nor turning."[31]

INTRODUCTION TO "THE CHRISTIAN UNIVERSALISM OF GEORGE FOX"

When I began to concentrate my studies on all the writings of George Fox more than forty years ago, it was during the period of Quaker history that might be called the "high tide" of the mystical interpretation of Quakerism. And when I had first encountered Fox's Journal just fifty years ago, I was not a professing Christian. If I had any bias when I read the Journal for the first time, it was in the direction of hoping to find in Fox the "perennial philosophy" of the mystics. But as I continued to study Fox, I became convinced that the great work on which he labored so faithfully all through his life was to preach the good news concerning Jesus Christ and how he saves people, and I became convinced of the truth of this gospel message.—Lewis Benson

"The Christian Universalism of George Fox" is the tenth and final lecture in the series *Rediscovering the Teaching of George Fox* that Lewis

---

30. Benson, "Church of the Cross," 48–49.
31. Fox, *Works*, 7:295.

Benson gave at the meetinghouse in Moorestown, New Jersey, in 1982. These lectures were prepared with those in mind who had been reached through hearing gospel ministry and, as a result, had wanted to "become involved in the work of preaching it again."[32] Each of the first eight lectures in this series covers a specific area of Fox's teaching. The final two lectures (this and the previous one, "Fox's Teaching on the Holy Spirit") were included to prepare those who will go out to preach the gospel, and who can expect to "run into questions about holy spirit religion and about non-Christian universalism."

In this essay, Benson distills significant points from various scholars' writings regarding the interface between universal mystical faith and Quakers. Rufus Jones figures prominently in this inventory, and Geoffrey Nuttall, Melvin B. Endy, and John Yungblut[33] are mentioned as well. Going beyond scholarly positions, however, Benson presents Fox's moving past intellectualism and into the wisdom of sequential, inward experience, which culminates in the knowledge of the inward Christ *as person* (i.e., having a face). The verse from 2 Corinthians 4:6, encapsulated in the following, was frequently referred to by Friends:

> Believers in Christ Jesus and the apostles and disciples . . . preach Christ the covenant of light among the Gentiles, and so bring them from the darkness to the light, from the power of Satan to God . . . and brought them inwardly to the light that shines in their hearts, to give them the knowledge of the glory of God in the face of Jesus Christ .[34]

A frequent charge from the earliest decades of the movement was that Quakers eliminated from their faith Jesus Christ "who dwelt in Galilee and Judea and was crucified, buried, and rose on the third day." Though Friends

---

32. *Epigraph.* Benson, "Christian Universalism," 58. Benson, "Christian Universalism," 58.

33. Rufus Jones (1863–1948) was a Quaker philosopher and writer who attempted to integrate Liberal theology with Quaker faith. He was an influential and active American Friend and was instrumental in founding American Friends Service Committee. Geoffrey Nuttall (1911–2007) was a British Congregational minister and scholar of seventeenth-century ecclesiastical history. He asserted there were essential links between Quakerism and Puritanism. Melvin B. Endy (b. 1938) is a Quaker scholar and author of *William Penn and Early Quakerism*. John Yungblut (1913–1995) was a student of Rufus Jones and was influenced by the writings of C. G. Jung. Yungblut emphasized the place of mysticism in Christianity.

34. Cadbury, *AC*, Cat. No 115E, 134–35 as quoted in Benson, "Christian Universalism," 60.

always denied the accusation, and owned Christ's "appearance of him in his body of flesh," they formally stated their position in "The Christian Doctrine of the People called Quakers Cleared."[35] Benson quotes from this document, which was prepared in 1694 by trusted ministers and leaders in the Society. Here is one statement from that document: "The son of God cannot be divided . . . nor is the sufficiency of his light within set up by us in opposition to him."[36]

Benson identifies a more recent challenge to the early Quaker message as "denominational-mindedness." The principle behind this thinking is that different "natures" require different philosophies or theologies, thus accounting for the many denominations. Since Benson's time, denominational-mindedness has gained ground among Quakers, and a diversity of philosophies is now seen as valid not only for those outside of the Society but for those within. A tightening conformity to the doctrine of individualism has accelerated the proliferation of ideologies within the Society. Resisted by most is the observation that human nature is intrinsic and universal, the same in every time and place, and that Jesus Christ speaks to this universal condition.

Benson concludes this lecture series with the following:

> [Early Quakers] were proclaiming that Christ, who is present in the midst of his people in all his offices, is the means that God has provided to save not just the Jews, or the Christians, but all people, all nations. The need today is for more men and women who are prepared to go forth and proclaim this gospel to Quakers, Christians, and people of all faiths, or none. "It is a wonderful thing to be called to the ministry of the gospel of Jesus Christ."[37]

---

35. Benson, "Christian Universalism," 60.
36. Benson, "Christian Universalism," 60.
37. Benson, "Christian Universalism," 61.

Dialogue on Quaker Understanding of Free Will

THIS IS A TRANSCRIPT of a dialogue between Stuart Masters and me that occurred in early to mid-December 2017 in the comment section of Stuart's blog post "Friends of Martin Luther? Quakers and the Protestant Reformation."[1] The point I challenged was Stuart's assertion that by a free act of will man participates in his transformation from sinner to saint. I contended early Quaker understanding held that the will is not free until liberated by Christ.

Patricia writes (quoting from Stuart's post):

> While people may be incapable of transforming themselves, humans have sufficient free will to make this fundamental choice, and when they do, by God's transformative power, it is possible for them to come into perfect conformity to the will of God (i.e., holiness or perfection).

Stuart, your stating that Quakers believed that "humans have sufficient free will to make this fundamental choice" is not accurate. Nayler writes:

> There is no will free for God but that which is free from sin, which will man lost in the fall, when he let in the will of the devil and entered into it; wherein man became in bondage. And all that man in that state knows of the free-will, is that which moves in him against the will of the flesh and of the devil, which is seen in the light of Christ.[2]

Man is either in the will of the devil or he is in the will of God, the latter moving in him against the will of the devil. There is no neutral state from

---

1. Masters, "Friends of Luther."
2. Nayler, *Works*, 3:133.

which man chooses the one or the other. To claim otherwise encourages "self-willed" man to remain self-satisfied, imagining himself in an innocuous, autonomous state, rather than his true state of being poor, helpless, blind, and naked, and without God.

Stuart writes:

Hi Pat,

Thank you for your comment! I am aware of this Nayler passage, which I think comes from "Love to the Lost." However, I cannot believe that Nayler means what you suggest he means.

Since early Friends rejected Calvinist double predestination, logically, they had to accept that there was a degree of human cooperation with God in the salvation process. They much have accepted the need for a human response to the divine offer. If not, there would have been no point launching the massive preaching campaign during the 1650s. The essential exhortation to turn away from carnal things and toward the light of Christ in the conscience, requires a response from its hearers.

I agree that they limited the extent of free will (and saw human willfulness as a key aspect of sin). However, no free will, no choice to turn to Christ, only God's action (which in this sense would have to be coercive, and against the free choice of the individual, which then leads to the problem of explaining why God might force this on some but not on others, bringing us back to the issue of predestination.)

Shalom,
Stuart.

Patricia writes:

I think if you read through the section titled "Concerning Free-Will" in "Love to the Lost," you will see that I am correct in saying that Nayler asserts there is either God's will or the devil's will, with no free will (in our contemporary understanding of the term as autonomy) that stands apart from the two. The passageway from one to the other is given through the quickening Word of God. Nayler writes:

> and as the spiritual man is quickened by the word of God, and that man born which is not of the flesh, nor of the will of it; so is that will seen again in man which is free, wherein the creature is made free from the will of the flesh, which is bondage.[3]

3. Nayler, *Works*, 3:133.

As it is not within man's ability to give birth to himself, it cannot be he who autonomously wills to be born from above; he is born of God. To be born of God occurs not from the will of the flesh, nor the will of man (John 1:13 [KJV]). It was the Word of God that seventeenth-century Friends preached, to the end that others could feel the quickening seed of God within (as they themselves had been given), and feeling that quickening they found entry into God's will, and thus experienced their freedom, which hitherto they had not known.

> So man hath not free-will further than he is free-born from above of the seed that sinneth not.[4]

Stuart writes:

My view has always been that the Early Quaker position was closer to that of Wesley than to Calvin. However, I need to be open to the possibility that their roots in Calvinist Puritanism left a legacy in their faith and practice.

My interpretation of Nayler's words are that he is emphasizing the view that salvation comes by the work of God alone and not by the effort of the individual. I agree with this and feel that it is consistent with the early Quaker position generally.

Early Friends were clearly very "black and white" in their understandings; one was either in darkness or in the light, in God's will or the devil's will, in the first birth or the second birth etc.... That need not imply that they did not feel that all people were faced with a choice; to turn to God or to remain in darkness. Such a choice presumes a degree (however limited) of free choice.

However, that does not resolve the very serious problem I outlined in my first response, which you have not answered. If humans have no free agency or choice in the salvation process, then we are left with the Calvinist positions of predestination and irresistible grace. This implies that God chooses some for salvation and others for damnation, without any human choice or decision.

I cannot accept that this was the message of the first Friends.

Shalom,
Stuart.

---

4. Nayler, *Works*, 3:134.

Dialogue on Quaker Understanding of Free Will

Patricia writes:

The Cain and Abel story offers information on how to understand Friends perspective on God's acceptance of man, or lack thereof. Following the telling of each brother's sacrifice, God's respect to Abel's but not to Cain's, and Cain's anger, He speaks:

> If thou doest well, shalt thou not be accepted? and if thou doest not well, sin lieth at the door (Gen 4:7).[5]

What is interesting here is God's speaking as though Cain knows what doing "well" entails and is not doing it. The text presents what appears to be identical behaviors between the two brothers: They both bring offerings of their labor, described with almost identical words, but only one's is accepted while the other's is not. We can't see what's amiss with Cain's offering, but God can and does, and furthermore knows Cain does as well, and holds him accountable. By having nearly identical descriptions of the brothers' sacrifices but God's judgment differing towards them, we see a narrative device by which the difference between the brothers is located: the difference between them lies within, invisible to us on the outside (and invisible to those who prefer darkness to light) but visible to God, who knows the heart.

Where has Cain failed? A strong clue is the word Jesus uses in Matthew 23:35 to describe his brother: "righteous Abel." God expects Cain (and each of us) to live up to the capacity given: first, to love truth/righteousness; second, to recognize our limits in knowing truth/righteousness; and third, to hunger and thirst after righteousness (Matt 5:6), that we might be filled. This love of truth requires an inward sacrifice, and Fox affirms Cain's lack of it when he wrote in "The Papist's Strength": "he [Cain] observed outward things, and comes not to witness the spiritual sacrifice."[6]

"I am sought of them that asked not for me; I am found of them that sought me not" (Isa 65:1) is a verse that points to the heeding of the seed of God within before it is known that there is such a thing; it is those who heed and love and seek a place to stand that only truth can provide; that mourn its lack with heart, mind, soul, and strength: it is these who come to be comforted through the mercy of God in his sending of his Spirit. It is not our choice or decision to suffer such need, but sensing its truth, we do not muffle or darken, obscure or deny, but instead, feelingly know the

---

5. King James Version, all subsequent citations are from this version.
6. Benson, *Notes,* R6 988.

emptiness of the heart, which cannot, should not, and will not be placated by any means at our disposal or will.

Stuart writes:

I am currently doing research for a book on James Nayler's theology and so will need to address this matter.

I agree that the work of salvation is God's work alone, and not about our personal effort, but maintain that, unless we at least have the freedom to respond to God's offer of salvation, we are left with the irresistible grace of Calvinism.

Early Friends, like many others, separated from their parish churches and were seekers of truth. That seems to imply an act of choice, even if it was divinely guided. Fox exhorts people not to quench the Spirit, which implies a decision not to follow its leadings. The very act of Adam's disobedience implies making a choice against the way of God.

If no-one has choice, no-one can be held responsible or accountable. They could do nothing else.

Patricia writes:

Your reasoning is sound, Stuart, but it starts from the wrong premise. We are not like a king who sits on a throne deciding and choosing what will be the law of his land: God's salvation or the devil's perfidy. Rather we are like a subject deep in a pit with no way out. It is not by choice or decision that we see our pitiful state, because, in truth, it is impossible not to see it—for those who have eyes to see. We do not choose to mourn our condition, as, in truth, it is impossible for a creature not to mourn its captivity—for those who have a heart that feels. "O wretched man that I am! who shall deliver me from this body of death? I thank God through Jesus Christ our Lord" (Rom 7:24–25). Paul is showing the necessity of seeing and feeling our true state, and the means of our deliverance. Truth, truth, truth from first to last, from captivity to freedom!

I've tried to show that there is another way to understand the solution to our condition other than (1) a participatory use of human will, or (2) election via the doctrine of predestination. I am convinced that it is the one understood by first Friends and is also in accord with Scriptures. I'm grateful for this opportunity to have discussed the issue with you.

May the love of Christ be with us.
Patricia

Dialogue on Quaker Understanding of Free Will

Stuart writes:

Thank you, Pat, I am certainly willing to take account of the perspective you have outline[d]. In any event, I need to do more work on this issue.
In the love of Christ,
Stuart

[The discussion continued one week later.]

Stuart writes:

Hi Pat,

I have been doing some research on how human "will" was understood in the early modern period. It seems that "will" primarily related to human to our emotions, motivation, and affections, rather than agency or the capacity to make choices. On this basis, I can agree with what you have said about the position of early Friends without rejecting my belief that Friends accepted that humans could make a choice about whether to respond to God's offer of regeneration and salvation.

Essentially, I think we were simply defining the term "free will" differently.

Shalom,
Stuart.

Patricia writes:

Stuart,

Your new definition of "will" does not affect the argument that there is no neutral ground from which to exercise free will, which is the position of first Friends, which I've explained. It is not possible to "choose," because the will is captivated until it is set free by Christ, the Truth. Here's Penington's clear refutation of the will standing of itself "free to both equally":

> But as for your speaking of free will, ye do not know what you speak of; for the will with the freedom of it, either stands in the image and power of him that made it, or in a contrary image and power.... [Mark this.] The will is not of itself, but stands in another, and is servant to that in whom it stands, and there its freedom is bound and comprehended. For there is no middle state between both, wherein the will stands of itself, and is free to both equally,

but it is a servant and under the command of one of these powers … such free will as men commonly speak of is mere imagination.⁷

Stuart writes:

Well we'll just have to agree to disagree on this issue.

*

On October 12, 2021, Patricia wrote:

Having asked Stuart's permission in August 2021 to include this dialogue on free will, I received the following response:

> I remember the exchange well and I am very happy for you to include it. Our dialogue led me to reconsider my position on Nayler's understanding of free will. In my recently published book on the theology of James Nayler (*The Rule of Christ: Themes in the Theology of James Nayler*, Brill, 2021), I argue that Nayler seems to hold either a monogystic or minimal synergistic view of the salvation process (i.e., that the most a human can do is surrender to God's work within them by the Holy Spirit, they are unable to do more than that themselves).

---

7. Penington, *Works*, 1:77.

Dialogue on Old Testament Stories

THIS POST IS A transcription of an email discussion that took place in mid-July 2020 with Ryan Hodges, a Christian from British Columbia who has been dissatisfied with nominal Christianity, and recently come across the writings of Quakers. In the following post, Ryan asks for information on early Friends position on the validity of the Old Testament atrocity stories, as he's found the way God is represented in those stories to be not in keeping with his understanding of God's character. A large portion of the second email exchange will focus on particular thoughts about the relationship between God and Man as represented in Scripture writings on covenants.

Thanks to Ryan for bringing up these ideas and also for his integrity of mind, which requires a seeking below the surface of doctrine for the reality of faith.

Ryan writes:

Do you believe that God commanded people to kill other people . . . ever? When David says, "Blessed is the one who bashes the brains out of Edomite infants" (Ps 137), do you believe that he was inspired of God to say this? I cannot see this as possible, my spirit recoils at the idea. Yet, murder and violence towards enemies is deeply embedded in the Old Testament narrative, and not just that people did it, but that the text specifically and often says God told them to do it. To say that this was somehow preparatory for the New Covenant, is to say that people "did evil, so that good may come." As of this point in time, I cannot swallow that idea. The same people that said, "God gave us this cultus to follow," also said "God often told us to commit genocide." Why should I trust such voices? Did the Prophets ever specifically endorse the cultus? I am not aware that they did. On the other hand, there seems like much evidence to suppose that they could have been "anti-cultus" altogether. This is a preliminary question for me in reading up to page 16 in Benson's "The Antipathy Between Prophecy and Religion."

I would like to hear your thoughts, or any other Quaker resources you may recommend that discuss this issue.

Patricia writes:

Ryan,

In your July 13th email, you wrote: "Do you believe that God commanded people to kill other people . . . ever?"

What early Friends ultimately sought in their reading of Scriptures was not lessons in history or ethics; what they found was information pertaining to God's nature and intention, as well as types, figures, and shadows that articulated the righteousness they were to embody and the sin they were to shun.

What does God's command "to kill other people" signify about God's intent and nature? One, it signifies God does not tolerate idolatry in people, and one had better "kill" whatever idolatry exists in one's own self, as formerly idolators were literally killed; two, if one chooses to persist in idolatry, God will not allow the soul to live; three, this life or death of the soul is a highly serious matter for human beings; four, the life of the body is not God's primary consideration but the life of the soul and what it worships. No doubt there are other lessons too. I'm just trying to show that Friends did not confine their interpretation to the literal meaning; their use of Scripture entailed more.

> I saw death reigned over them from Adam to Moses, from the entrance into transgression till they came to the ministration of condemnation, which restrains people from sin that brings death. Then, when the ministration of Moses is passed through, the ministry of the prophets comes to be read and understood, which reaches through the figures, types and shadows unto John, the greatest prophet born of woman; whose ministration prepares the way of the Lord by bringing down the exalted mountains and making straight paths. And as this ministration is passed through, an entrance comes to be known into the everlasting kingdom.[1]

Here is a passage taken from Fox's journal, showing salvation history through time. Friends held that this grand-scale history was to be gone through by each person. I wrote more about moving beyond literal interpretation in an essay titled "That They All May Be One."[2] That said, it was

---

1. Nickalls, *Journal*, 31.
2. Dallmann, *Word Within*, 65.

also Friends understanding that Scriptures could not be read and understood except in the spirit in which they were written, which underscores Christ's admonition to seek first the kingdom and righteousness, and all things else will be given as well.

Ryan writes:

In reading your email and your attached blog post (which I really enjoyed), I have this to respond [to this statement of yours]: "What early Friends ultimately sought in their reading of Scriptures was not lessons in history or ethics." So what was their take on the historical validity of the stories themselves? Doubtful? Possible? Accurate? Why do I ask this? Because I wonder if it is acceptable to use stories of genocide, even symbolically, to express the nature of God's action in the world, or in the heart. It is fine not to take the stories "merely" as history, but should we not question whether the stories are historically possible with what we understand to be the character of God?

Patricia writes:

I have no recollection of reading that any of the early Friends thought that the Old Testament atrocity stories were anything but accurate. I don't find them contrary to what I understand to be the nature of God to move humanity incrementally forward over the millennia from a condition that is brutal, violent, and lawless, and into the kingdom. There is great variation in the readiness to receive Christ among individual souls; God takes figuratively withered, cast forth branches and consigns them to the figurative fire (John 15:6), or the Flood. Matthew 10:28 (KJV) illustrates where the concern of God and his Christ is placed:

> And fear not them which kill the body, but are not able to kill the soul: but rather fear him which is able to destroy both soul and body in hell.

Dialogue on the Import of Covenants

SEVERAL DAYS LATER, RYAN continued our discussion:

I am uncomfortable with the idea of "ministrations," or as the rest of Christendom calls them: "dispensations." This is what is always claimed about the genocidal stories of the Old Testament: "that was a different dispensation (ministration); God doesn't deal with people in that way anymore. God wouldn't ask us to commit genocide these days." I cannot reconcile that idea with an unchanging God. This idea of dispensations (I believe) comes from a misunderstanding of the concept of a "New Covenant." The idea of a new vs. old covenant was something that could be relevant to Jews in the time of Jesus/Paul, because they had actually lived under the Sinai covenant. Gentiles such as us were never under such a covenant. It seems nonsensical to me that Christians say, "We aren't under the law anymore," when we, nor our forefathers ever did live under such a law/old covenant. All we have ever had the option of, was the covenant as we have been offered through Jesus. How does "being under the law" mean anything to us gentiles? "New" in the Hebrew language holds the meaning of "fresh/vital" in it; it is not strictly and exclusively used as something that must be juxtaposed with something old. I think this is one of the jumping off points of getting into the whole "dispensations/ministrations" idea. It's ok in a certain sense for Jews of Jesus's day to discuss the Old vs. New covenants, but for a gentile? I can't see the sense in that.

Patricia writes:

You say you cannot reconcile the idea of different dispensations with "an unchanging God." God doesn't change his nature or intent; time, however, is the medium of change, and we, his creatures who inhabit time, manifest different/changing situations. God's response to these situations will vary to the effect that his one unchanging intent is furthered and met: the kingdom of God "on earth as it is in heaven."

As for what does "being under the law" mean to us gentiles, I can think of a couple of things. First, in my Protestant religious training, the ten commandments were studied as God's law, which we were to follow. Second, the idea of the authority of law is a hallmark of Western Civilization, and it can be traced back to the sacred authority allotted to God's law as given to the Hebrews. Other societies had authoritarian strong men (such as Egypt's Pharaoh) who ruled as they pleased with no authority (law) higher than themselves. This arrangement is typical not only of societies but also individuals where the "man of sin . . . sitteth in the temple of God, shewing himself that he is God."[1] Our civilization is one that recognizes the value of and is therefore regulated by law: international, national, state or province, and local. We all know what it means to be subject to law, and we get that principle from the Hebrews. So, when we get something new—something beyond the outward, socio-political law—to regulate our lives, we contrast the new way with the old way of obedience to the law. We know the old way of regulation—laws and principles—and when we are given the Christ, the living law in the heart, we know that this is the new and living way.

Ryan writes:

The fresh/vital covenant is not something I see as initiated by Jesus, but he was a proponent of it. Adam had at least an opportunity to embrace it. Cain was counselled by God to embrace it. Enoch walked in it. Abraham found it "coming to the mountain on the third day." Melchizedek seems to have been a priest in its ways. David wrote songs extolling its virtues. The prophets felt it, possibly walked in it, and encouraged others to embrace it. I don't see this fresh/vital covenant as exclusively appearing after Jesus's death and resurrection.

Patricia writes:

Christ is the new covenant, meaning he mediates the relationship between God and his people. Jesus Christ is not a time-bound, worldly creature, such as is the unredeemed man who is the first Adam; Christ is the second Adam: not man but the Son of man; his life is not time-bound

---

1. 2 Thess 2:3–4 (King James Version, all subsequent citations are taken from this version).

but is eternal. He asserts this difference when he says to the Jews: "Before Abraham was, I am" (John 8:58). Yet, as a Galilean, he was also within time and ministering to the unredeemed, time-bound creatures around him that they might know God and Jesus Christ whom he has sent, which is eternal life (John 17:3). In his time-bound (historical) existence, he exemplifies our being which can (like his own) transcend our captivity within time (and thus subjection to death) and enter into the freedom of the eternal, while we yet are on earth. Hebrew prophets knew of this being who would appear in time and mediate between the natural, time-bound nature and the eternal; yet although they had borne witness to the Light, they were not that Light (John 1:7–9, Deut 18:15). They had not claimed that they and the Father were one, nor that we could be one with the Father as he was one with the Father (John 17:21). We, too, are one with the Father through Christ, our mediator, just as two parties in a covenant figuratively become one.

Ryan writes:

What was Jesus, while walking on this earth in the flesh, encouraging people to embrace in that "here and now" 2000 years ago? When he says in John:

> John 5:24: Truly, truly, I say unto you, He that heareth my word and believeth on him that sent me hath eternal life, and shall not come into condemnation; but is passed from death to life.

He doesn't say they "will have" eternal life. He says they do have it, he doesn't say they "will not" come into judgement, but that they "do not" come into judgement, he doesn't say they "will pass" from death into life, but that they "have passed" from death into life. He didn't say these things as impending promises to be ratified after his death and resurrection and coming in spirit, he speaks of these things as present realities at the moment he spoke them. Why is this? As I understand it, it is because the "new" in the "new covenant" should not be understood as "new vs. old" but it should be understood as "fresh/vital".

He also states: "All who have learned from God, come to me." And "If you had known God you would have known me." Do we put the cart in front of the horse in saying we must know Jesus in order to know God? Isn't Jesus's point this: All who know what God is like will recognize me as coming from that God that they have already come to have known in some way? This "coming to have known God in some way," I see has only taken

Dialogue on the Import of Covenants

place through the power of God's ultimate covenant, his speaking directly to the heart of the individual.

Patricia writes:

I agree that "that which may be known of God is manifest in [us] for God hath shewed it unto [us]" (Rom 1:19) and think the same idea is present in John 6:44: "No man can come to me, except the Father which hath sent me draw him: and I will raise him up at the last day."

Ryan writes:

The thing that is often left out of these Old/New covenant discussions is the covenant that God made with Abraham, the covenant "of the pieces" in Genesis 15, this is God's covenant of promise to Abraham in which he blesses Abraham's descendants. This is the covenant promise that Paul speaks of, and of which Paul states that the "law" coming in 430 years later, cannot annul. In this sense the Sinai "covenant" is not truly the "first covenant" and it is not the covenant of God that he holds with the "faithful." The law is not of faith, those who followed the law were to have life in keeping the commandments of that law, but that in no way abrogates the earlier covenant of promise made to Abraham and his "faith descendants." Faith was a concept clarified in the life of Abraham, so he was the model of faith for those who would come after him, that does not mean that God's covenant with those of faith did not exist before that time. I think Enoch is a perfect example of this "faith/new/fresh/vital covenant." He walked with God, that's it, that is all we know. And through walking with God, "he was not, for God took him." Is this not what we are talking about when we talk about the cross? "losing your life to find it?" "taking up your cross and following?" Is this not the beating heart of the New Covenant as Jesus taught it?

In the end I will mention that the Concept of the New Covenant, as is understood by Catholics, Protestants, and Quakers alike, is strongly influenced by the "letter to the Hebrews," and that this letter has a long history of being of questionable reliability in church history. "Should it be included in the cannon?" "Are the concepts included in it worthy of the greater vision of Scriptures?" That isn't to say that there are not worthy ideas in it, but I believe that if it preaches a unique idea that is difficult to fit with the rest of the Scriptures, that unique idea should be held under close scrutiny.

Patricia writes:

Let's work on the question about Hebrews another time.

What Jeremiah identifies as the new covenant to come is the Lord's putting his law in the inward parts, and writing "it in their hearts" (Jer 31:33). It is a relationship that is characterized by subjection to the Lord our Righteousness. Some willingly subject themselves to the inwardly known right and true, such as Abraham and other prophets (and those who "hunger and thirst after righteousness" [Matt 5:6]), and thus heed the drawings of the holy Spirit (John 6:44); most do not. In John 21:20, the beloved disciple, John, is shown to have sought out the truth of his inward state, and thereby had subjected himself to the truth in the inward parts; whereas Peter in this chapter is shown to have needed some discipline and was reminded several times that his actions/character weren't acceptable. (For more explanation of this comparison of John and Peter, see the next to the last segment (titled "Preparation for the Work of Restoration") in my essay "To Stand Still in the Light."[2]

When Jesus says "And I, if I be lifted up from the earth, will draw all men unto me" (John 12:32), he is anticipating the effect his dying upon the cross will have upon humanity. The historical cross is an example of man's obedience to God's intent/command, even unto the death. Through example, Jesus models to unredeemed man the necessity of obedience to God, and thereby the necessity of crucifying the worldly, self-serving life. As a visible act in history, the cross teaches us by example in a way that words might not. Some—the prophets and seers of all ages and places—already have known the inward process, the dying to the self that precedes receiving faith. But Jesus wasn't interested in just a few; the Father's Will was that "all men" (John 12:32) be drawn unto Christ Jesus and into his kingdom. Therefore, obedience unto death, and resurrection to new life, was enacted, and thus, as a figure or type of the inward process, shows the way to all.

These are very difficult ideas to express. I think the closer one keeps to the inward experience of what all the imagery and history portends, the more accurate one's ideas can be. I hope my explanations have reached a place of understanding in you, as they may require as much effort on your part as they have on mine.

---

2. Dallmann, *Word Within*, 17–19.

A Conversation on Faith

THE FOLLOWING IS A copy of an email exchange that occurred May 4–6, 2021, between Madeleine Vaché and me. Madeleine has been attending a New Foundation Fellowship (NFF) Fox study group, as well as a Zoom Bible study and classes on early Friends beliefs offered under the care of Ohio Yearly Meeting (Conservative): classes I also attend. She begins her correspondence by referring to an essay by Lewis Benson titled "The Future of Quakerism."[1] Benson, along with several others, founded New Foundation Fellowship (NFF) half a century ago to be a vehicle for presenting the writing of Fox to modern Friends, who had wandered far from the original faith. His work was to proclaim and speak of "Jesus Christ, the same yesterday, and to day, and for ever."[2]

Madeleine writes:

Dear Patricia,

As an introduction to Lewis Benson's work I am reading *None Were So Clear* (nice to see you and the Hein's acknowledged). In the lecture on "The Future of Quakerism," he describes much of modern Liberal Friends' thought and states it more clearly than anyone I've read before: I find your answers to questions to be deep and wise, so I'm addressing mine to you.

> The religion of the modern Friend is a philosophical structure whose chief cornerstone is the affirmation of the inherent native spirituality of man. This is what the modern Friend means when he uses George Fox's phrase "that of God in every man." . . . Christ, or rather Jesus, is understood to be a rabbi who taught that we must follow our Inner Light. . . . He is not the Light, but he

---

1. Wallace, *None*, 42–59.
2. Heb 13:8 (King James Version; all subsequent citations are taken from this version).

received it in the same manner we do. Thus, the Inner Light is one thing and Jesus is another.[3]

I think somewhere else in the essay he indicates that modern Friends no longer see the necessity of Christ as intermediary between God and man.

The support for this modern belief seems to come, as well, from early and current-day Quakers' universalism, saying that the Inner Light existed in all people well before Jesus and exists within everyone. My question is this: What were the early "evangelists" doing when they traveled as far as Turkey to talk with a Sultan or when Fox encouraged Friends to speak with American Indians? Were they saying that the full expression of the Light required familiarity with or acceptance of the direct teachings of Jesus? Did they believe that only with that could the Light be fully present or active? Another way to ask this is, can there be two legitimate tracks for Friends, one that relies on Christ as both message and messenger and another that relies on a shared sense of the presence of the Light?

I think that Benson goes on in that lecture to say, basically, that the second form of belief is anemic, that it won't support an eternal fellowship in the same way the first one does. The argument against that might be (within a very time-limited framework) that modern Liberal thought seems to be more robust and attractive than the Benson version. It's a small group, of course, but all mainline denominations are. And the reply to that is yes, of course, they're small because they've lost nearly everything of early Christianity to secularism.

Well, I will be interested to see your reply if you have the time. I want you to know that I am still interested in the Fox studies, though I believe that I have a conflict again this Saturday. I'll be certain to listen to the session when you post it in *Abiding Quaker*, which I greatly appreciate.

In grace, Madeleine

Patricia writes:

Thank you for writing and for posing these questions, Madeleine. I've often felt that your questions in our Fox study groups show a seriousness and an intelligence that is welcome. I've been considering your email since first reading it yesterday and feel I may be able to shed some light, though perhaps not fully clear up the matter for you. If that's the case, please let me know, and I'll try again.

---

3. Wallace, *None*, 51.

A Conversation on Faith

You had asked about the evangelical work of early Quakers to non-Christian people, such as the sultan in Turkey and the American Indians: whether in evangelizing, Friends were saying that "the full expression of the Light required familiarity with or acceptance of the direct teachings of Jesus . . . that only with that could the Light be fully present or active?" Barclay in his sixth proposition in his *Apology*[4] refutes that idea when he states "that some of the old philosophers might have been saved, so also may now some—who by providence are cast into those remote parts of the world, where the knowledge of the history is wanting—be made partakers of the divine mystery, if they receive and resist not that grace, 'a manifestation whereof is given to every man to profit withal'" (1 Cor 12:7). He goes on to identify where the true distinguishing event of salvation lies: "they may be made partakers of the mystery of his death (though ignorant of the history) *if they suffer his Seed and Light, enlightening the hearts, to take place*; in which Light, communion with the Father and Son is enjoyed." (Italics are mine.) Verses 9 through 12 in the prologue of John likewise state that the light is universally given but not universally received.

Benson recognized that modern Friends—for the most part—had not entered in at the strait gate, had not received the Light of Christ but instead had misconstrued the relationship between Christ Jesus and themselves. As he wrote in the passage you quoted, they attributed the divine nature to themselves as an "inherent" function of their human nature. It is this claim of a natural inherency that stands in opposition to original Quaker faith. Early Quakers received Christ, knowing his being to be wholly other than themselves, having a different will and wisdom beyond their natural human capacity but which, nevertheless, could visit, enlighten, and direct them. Benson picks up on Fox's use of the idea of "the offices of Christ" which emphasizes the distinction between Christ and human beings, who yet, though distinct from one another, can be in relationship: one entity to another.

Modern Friends sometimes claim to be in unity with early Friends and feel entitled to use the same terms to describe their spirituality, but the way in which they use these terms shows that their understanding is different from early Friends. For example, a modern Friend believes he possesses his own unique "inner light," which "leads" him in ways that differ from the ways others' unique inner lights lead them. For early Friends, the Light of Christ is not a personal possession, and one cannot control whether or not

---

4. Barclay, *Apology*, 96–97.

it shines within. They felt and knew Christ reveal himself to them within. This specific revelation brought them into unity with others who likewise felt the same being descend upon them from above; Fox wrote: "your faith being in the power you are all one if ye be 10,000."[5] Unity in Christ, arising from an inward conviction, engendered an assurance and strength both in individuals and in the corporate body that is evident in their writings and history. They had a clarity, power, and unity which is non-existent in modern Quakers, leading Benson to use the term "anemic" to describe what the Society has come to.

In your email you asked, "can there be two legitimate tracks for Friends, one that relies on Christ as both message and messenger and another that relies on a shared sense of the presence of the Light?" Perhaps the previous paragraph has answered this already in presenting the idea that a legitimate shared sense of the Light will occur only upon the visitation from Christ, the transcendent Being. Unity can be engineered by human means, but it is not the unity of spirit that is revealed from heaven, which exhibits a specific quality of grace and truth that leads those who have known it into a unity with one another. This unity extends beyond the people gathered in a particular space; it is found among those from different times and cultures, allowing us to read and understand the Scriptures, understanding them as did the early Friends, because we know—as they knew—the Spirit of Christ in which the Scriptures were written. Modern Friends tend to avoid the Scriptures, whereas early Friends highly valued both the Scriptures and the Spirit they spoke of; they knew and loved that Spirit, in which they lived and moved and had their being (Acts 17:28).

Please let me know if this response has sufficiently clarified the matter, or if not, feel free to pursue it further.
Patricia

Madeleine writes:

Dear Patricia,

This was most helpful, and I appreciate the time you took to think it through and write back to me.

The main question that remains for me, the larger body aside, is about receiving Christ. About thirty years ago I had a "born again" moment in which, in accepting Christ, I was promised abundant and eternal life. As satisfying as that was, I recognize that receiving Christ is not a one-time

---

5. Fox, *Works*, 7:58.

event. Since I first heard of it, when I was young, I was moved by the instruction to "pray without ceasing." I am still trying to understand what it takes to maintain that connection: some study (I know Scripture is important), willingness, openness, desire, paring away of distractions, or . . . something. How do you see that continued work? How do you listen for Christ's leadings? Are there early Friends who speak of it and might help me expand into that state?

With much gratitude,

Madeleine

Patricia writes:

Dear Madeleine,

I appreciate your writing of your present condition and doing so in such a concise, essential way. My condition mirrors your own: I was given knowledge of God several decades ago, and since that time, have been striving to "maintain that connection." To live in the fear of God is one principle that has become a part of me. It is within our human capacity to sustain and is usually present, a consequence of knowing and desiring life: a spiritual survival "instinct." Like an instinct, the fear alerts me to situations where I'm spiritually endangered. It preserves me, keeping me safe from sin that would take my life. But that's all it does; as an embodied principle, fear of God doesn't and can't precipitate the bestowal of grace, as grace is God's alone to give.

You also asked how I listen for Christ's leadings. I am open to being judged, knowing what has prevented my receiving him are my natural—perhaps unseen—shortcomings, sometimes subconsciously hidden so that I'm unaware of them. To get these errors visible, I open myself to receive any information that I've kept hidden away from sight; I trust God to reveal whatever is necessary and to sustain me through the indictment, as I've experienced this process so many, many times. Listening also requires focus, and one technique I find helpful is to repeat the Lord's prayer at the beginning of worship, one phrase at a time, allowing each one to deepen and focus my attention. Following that exercise, I simply wait, alert and scanning the inward horizon for signs of any movement of the Spirit.

Having friends who are honest and dedicated to the same goal is helpful, for the obvious reason that having another's perspective can add information and understanding. Reading of Scripture and early Friends writings are useful for the same reason. I like Isaac Penington's writings for his sensitivity to and articulation of the inward workings of mind and heart. His four-volume *Works* are available from Quaker Heritage Press, and Friends Library has published a two-volume set of his *Works*, "conscientiously abridged." Here's an example of Penington's insightful writing taken from a treatise that is titled "Some Questions and Answers, Conducing Towards the Further Manifestation and Opening of the Path of Redemption and Eternal Life to the Eye of Spiritual Israel": [6]

> Now the more the spirit is broken by the hand of the Lord, and taught thereby to fear him; and the less strength it hath in itself, to grapple with the persecuting spirit of the world; the fitter it is to stand in God's counsel, to wait for his strength and preservation, which is able to bear up its head above all the rage and swelling of the waters of the worldly spirit in the men of this world.

Thanks again for sharing your interest and progress in these matters. I look forward to engaging in joint efforts in the work with you.

Patricia

Madeleine writes:

Dear Patricia,

Once again I feel deeply heard and attended to. You have set before me a banquet.

Madeleine

---

6. Penington, *Works*, 2:249.

Review of *Traditional Quaker Christianity*

As I read and re-read *Traditional Quaker Christianity*,[1] I felt a spirit of humble diligence intent upon conveying the core substance of Quaker understanding, as well as the practices that have thus far assisted its continuation. The original draft of this book was the result of a study of Friends faith and witness by Ohio Yearly Meeting (Conservative) member Michael Hatfield. He gave his work to the yearly meeting "to do with as it saw fit." Small study groups were formed in which his writing was found useful but in need of more work. The yearly meeting called upon four Friends (Arthur Berk, John Smith, Susan Smith, and Terry Wallace) to edit and develop Hatfield's original draft.

There are seven chapters in the book, each containing anywhere from four to ten sections. Each section is comprised of a title, selections for recommended reading, a short essay, and questions for discussion. Four appendices complete the main body of the book, providing more discussion of eldering, a brief history and present-day scope of alternate forms of Quaker faith, a glossary of Quaker terms, and a bibliography.

This book would be helpful for anyone wanting a readable introduction to or comprehensive overview of the original tenets of Quaker Christianity, and the sustaining practices that have evolved in Ohio Yearly Meeting. The primary doctrines of the faith are all included: the Word of God is Christ (not the Bible); the Spirit of Christ is universally bestowed; salvation entails obedience to the living God (not intellectual assent to doctrine); only in the daily cross of Christ can evil be overcome. In addition to presenting the central beliefs, the book examines particular tenets that have arisen from the faith: that gospel ministry is oracular, that the Scriptures are esteemed and studied, that baptism and communion are inward occurrences, and that females and males have equal spiritual potential in

---

1. Berk et al., *Traditional Quaker Christianity*.

substance and practice. Pertinent passages from the Scriptures and Friends writings are frequently cited and paraphrased to supplement the editors' descriptions and explanations.

Some present-day misconstructions of Quaker faith are addressed. For example, in the fourth section of the first chapter, Lewis Benson is quoted contrasting the ethic of obligation with the ethic of idealism: the former being a principle grounded in divine Will as opposed to the latter, which is based in human values. A later discussion in chapter 7 on testimony versus testimonies furthers the discussion, and the difference is then illustrated in later sections where the original peace witness and the contemporary peace testimony are each described.

I found the essay on clerking substantial in identifying gifts needed for clerking, responsibilities of both clerk and meeting while conducting business, and helpful practical advice for maintaining order and writing or modifying a minute. Throughout the book, practical advice is regularly offered and always purposeful.

The roles of elders, overseers, ministers, and teachers are each described: their work, the strengths and gifts necessary, and the typical dangers encountered. A chart at the end of chapter 6 compares the different functions and orientations of each, providing an easy reference to Friends who are not practiced in identifying these gifts and are unfamiliar with their specific benefits to the community.

Though *Traditional Quaker Christianity* is intended to convey the tradition among Conservative Friends, it may find readers among Liberals and Evangelicals. Should another generation of Quakers come forth and undertake the restoration of "the desolations of many generations," they could find this book a resource for building up a Quaker Christian society. Here they would find stated the purpose and aim of the Society; means to realize that aim; practices to support those means; and generally, a structure provided in which a people of God could arise, flourish, and serve the cause of Truth.

Bibliography

Arendt, Hannah. *The Life of the Mind*. New York: Harcourt, Brace, Jovanovich, 1978.
Augustine. *The Confessions of St. Augustine*. Translated by Rex Warner. New York: Mentor, 1963.
Barclay, Robert. *Apology for the True Christian Divinity*. Glenside, PA: Quaker Heritage, 2002.
Barth, Karl. *Epistle to the Romans*. 6th ed. Oxford: Oxford University Press, 1968.
Benson, Lewis. *Catholic Quakerism*. Philadelphia: Philadelphia Yearly Meeting, 1968.
———. *A New Foundation to Build On*. https://storage.ning.com/topology/rest/1.0/file/get/657607615?profile=original.
———. *Notes on George Fox*. Moorestown, N.J., New Foundation, 1981.
———. *Rediscovering the Teachings of George Fox*. http://storage.ning.com/topology/rest/1.0/file/get/1115043257?profile=original.
———. *The Truth is Christ*. Gloucester, England: New Foundation, 1981.
Berk, Arthur, Jack Smith, Susan Smith, and T.H.S. Wallace, eds. *Traditional Quaker Christianity*. Barnesville, Ohio: Ohio Yearly Meeting, 2014.
Brunner, Emil. *The Christian Doctrine of the Church, Faith, and the Consummation*. Philadelphia: Westminster, 1960.
———. *The Christian Doctrine of Creation and Redemption*. 12th ed. Philadelphia: Westminster, 1974.
———. *Christianity and Civilisation*. New York: Chas. Scribner's Sons, 1949.
Dallmann, Patricia. *Abiding Quaker* (blog). patradallmann.com.
———. *The Word Within*. Camp Hill, PA: New Foundation, 2009.
Dickens, Charles. *Pictures from Italy*. London: Penguin, 1998.
Duvall, J. Scott. "Angry at Death: Reading John 11," *Intersections*, January 24, 2017, www.cbhd.org/intersections/angry-at-death-reading-john-11.
Fox, George. *The Works of George Fox*. Philadelphia: Marcus C. Gould, 1831.
Gaer, Joseph. *What the Great Religions Believe*. New York: Signet, 1964.
Howgill, Francis. *Some of the Mysteries of God's Kingdom Declared*. Wadsworth, Ohio: Friends Library, 2019.
Market Street Fellowship (MSF). *The Narrow Path* (listserv). https://marketstreetfellowship.com/.
Masters, Stuart. *A Quaker Stew* (blog). https://aquakerstew.blogspot.com/2017/11/friends-of-martin-luther-quakers-and_29.html.
Maurer, Johan. *Can You Believe?* (blog). https://blog.canyoubelieve.me/2018/12/what-makes-church-trustworthy-seeking.html.

Bibliography

McReynolds, Paul R., ed., *Word Study Greek-English New Testament*. Wheaton, IL: Tyndale House, 1998.

Molinos, Miguel, Jeanne-Marie Guyon, and Francois Fenelon. *A Guide to True Peace*, facsimile of 1815 edition compiled by William Backhouse and James Janson. Sebastopol, CA: Jim Wilson, 2019.

Nayler, James. *The Works of James Nayler*. Farmington, ME: Quaker Heritage, 2003–2009.

Nickalls, John L., ed. *The Journal of George Fox*. London: London Yearly Meeting of the Religious Society of Friends, 1985.

Palmer, G. E. H., Philip Sherrard, and Kallistos Ware, eds. *The Philokalia: The Complete Text*. Faber and Faber, 1983.

Penington, Isaac. *The Works of Isaac Penington*. Glenside, PA: Quaker Heritage, 1995–1997.

Pierpoint, Folliot S. "For the Beauty of the Earth." In *The Methodist Hymnal*, 35. Nashville, TN: The Methodist Publishing House, 1966.

Shewen, William. *Meditations and Experiences*. Market Street Fellowship Early Quakers Series, 2015. https://marketstreetfellowship.com/1185/book/meditations-and-experiences/.

Skinner, Max, and Gardiner Stillwell, eds. *That Thy Candles May Always Be Burning*. Camp Hill, PA: New Foundation, 2001.

Spielberg, Steven, dir. *Schindler's List*. Amblin Entertainment, Universal Pictures, 1994.

Stringfellow, William. *An Ethic for Christians & Other Aliens in a Strange Land*. Waco, TX: Word, 1973.

Strong, Mary, ed. *Letters of the Scattered Brotherhood*. San Francisco: HarperCollins, 1974.

von Trotta, Margarethe, dir. *Hannah Arendt*. New York: Heimatfilm, Zeitgeist 2012.

Wallace, T.H.S., ed. *None Were So Clear*. Camp Hill, PA: New Foundation, 1996.

Wall Street Journal editorial board. "He Is a Dictator." *WSJ* January 26, 2020. https://www.wsj.com/articles/he-is-a-dictator-11580075066.

www.ingramcontent.com/pod-product-compliance
Lightning Source LLC
Chambersburg PA
CBHW071429160426
43195CB00013B/1856